Acknowledgments, *xi*
Together We Prepare, *xvi*
    How to Use This Book, *xvi*
    Organization, *xvii*
Training, *xviii*
Automated External Defibrillation and the
    Cardiac Chain-of-Survival, *xviii*
Emergency Action Steps, *xx*
First Aid Kit, *xxi*

■ PART ONE: INJURY PREVENTION

General Principles to Prevent Injury, *2*
Coaching Responsibilities, *2*
Preseason Medical Examination, *2*
Guidelines for the Medical Approval/Examination, *4*
Emergency Action Plan, *5*
Checking the Facility Area, *7*
    Guidelines To Provide a Safe Environment, *8*
Equipment Selection and Use, *9*
    Guidelines for Equipment Selection and Use, *10*
Supervising Athletes, *12*
    Guidelines for Appropriate Supervision, *12*
    Guidelines for Parents, *13*
    Guidelines for Working Effectively with Parents, *14*
Preventing Further Injury, *15*
    Guidelines for Preventing Further Injury, *16*
Injury Prevention Checklist, *16*
Preventing Specific Injuries, *17*
    Head, Neck and Back Injuries, *17*
    Recognizing Spinal Injury, *18*
    Guidelines to Prevent Spinal Injury, *19*
Muscle, Bone and Joint (Musculoskeletal) Injuries, *19*
Warm-Up/Cool-Down, *19*
    Guidelines for Warm-Up/Cool-Down Activities, *21*
Training Methods, *22*
    Guidelines for Training, *22*

Preventing Overuse Injuries, 23
　　Guidelines to Prevent Overuse Injuries, 25
Other Emergencies, 25
Preventing Heat-Related Emergencies, 25
　　Guidelines to Prevent Heat-Related Emergencies, 26
Preventing Cold-Related Emergencies, 27
　　Guidelines to Prevent Hypothermia, 27
　　Guidelines to Prevent Frostbite, 28
Preventing Weather-Related Injuries, 29
　　Guidelines to Prevent Weather-Related Injuries, 29
Preventing Dehydration, 31
　　Guidelines to Prevent Dehydration, 31
　　Guidelines for Rehydration, 32
Preventing Nutritional Abuse and Eating Disorders, 32
　　Guidelines to Prevent Nutritional Abuse and Eating
　　　　Disorders, 35
Allergic Reactions, 37
Exercise-Induced Asthma, 38
Preventing Substance Abuse, 38
　　Guidelines to Prevent Substance Abuse, 40
Psychological Injuries, 42
　　Guidelines to Prevent Psychological Injuries, 43
Preventing Disease Transmission when
Giving Care, 43
　　Cleaning up a Blood or Body Fluid Spill, 46
　　Hepatitis B (HBV) Transmission, 47
　　Hepatitis C (HCV) Transmission, 48
　　Human Immunodeficiency Virus (HIV) Transmission, 48
After an Injury Occurs, 49
Return-To-Play Guidelines, 49
　　Guidelines for Return to Play, 49
Reporting and Documenting Injuries, 51
Transporting an Injured Athlete, 52
　　Guidelines for Transporting or Moving Injured Athletes, 52
Critical Incident Stress Debriefing, 53
　　Guidelines to Cope with Critical Incident Stress, 54
National Governing Bodies, 57
Emergency Care Permission Form (Sample), 61

American Red Cross

Together, we can save a life

36 USC 380

INJURY PREVENTION AND CARE
HANDBOOK

StayWell

StayWell

04 05 06 07 08 09 / 9 8 7 6 5 4 3 2 1

Instructions for Emergency Telephone Calls, 62
Information for Emergency Call, 63
Sample Incident Report Form, 64

■ PART TWO: EMERGENCY REFERENCE

Emergency Action Steps, 68
Abdominal Injury, 69
Abdominal Pain or Discomfort, 71
Abdominal Thrusts (see Choking—Conscious Adult or Child Athlete, p. 125)
Abrasion (see Wounds—Abrasion, p. 180)
Airway Obstruction (see Choking—Conscious Adult or Child Athlete, p. 125)
Allergic Reactions, 72
Amputation (see Wounds—Amputation/Avulsion, p. 181)
Animal Bite (see Bites and Stings—Animal Bite, p. 78)
Asthma (see Breathing Emergencies—Asthma, p. 90)
Athlete (see Checking An Unconscious Athlete—Adult or Child Athlete, p. 103)
Automated External Defibrillation (AED) (see Checking an Unconscious Athlete—AED, p. 118)
Bandaging, 75
Bites and Stings—Animal Bite, 78
Bites and Stings—Bee Sting, 79
Bites and Stings—Human Bite, 80
Bites and Stings—Insect Bite, 81
Bites and Stings—Marine Life Sting, 82
Bites and Stings—Scorpion Sting, 83
Bites and Stings—Snake Bite, 84
Bites and Stings—Spider Bite, 85
Bites and Stings—Tick Bite, 86
Bleeding (see Wounds—Bleeding, p. 182)
Bone or Joint Injury (see Muscle, Bone and Joint [Musculoskeletal] Injuries, p. 147)
Breathing Difficulty, 88
Breathing Emergencies—Asthma, 90
Breathing Emergencies—Hyperventilation, 93

Breathing—Stopped *(see Checking an Unconscious Athlete—Rescue Breathing—Adult or Child, p. 105)*

Broken Bone *(see Muscle, Bone and Joint (Musculoskeletal) Injuries, p. 147)*

Bruise *(see Wounds—Bruise, p. 185)*

Burns—Heat/Thermal, *94 (see also Burns—Chemical (p. 98) and Burns—Electrical (p. 99).*

Burns—Chemical, *98*

Burns—Electrical, *99*

Burns—Sunburn, *100*

Checking an Athlete for Consciousness—Adult or Child, *101*

Checking an Unconscious Athlete—Adult or Child, *103*

Checking an Unconscious Athlete—Rescue Breathing—Adult or Child, *105*

Checking an Unconscious Athlete—CPR—Adult (age 9 and older), *109*

Checking an Unconscious Athlete—CPR—Child (ages 1 to 8), *111*

Checking an Unconscious Athlete—Choking—Unconscious Adult or Child, *114*

Checking an Unconscious Athlete—Automated External Defibrillation (AED)—Using an AED on an Adult (age 9 or older), *118*

Checking an Unconscious Athlete—Automated External Defibrillation (AED)—Using an AED on a Child (ages 1 to 8), *120*

Cheek Injury *(see Mouth and Jaw Injury, p. 144)*

Chest Injury *(see Wounds—Chest Injuries, p. 185)*

Chest Pain or Pressure/Possible Heart Attack, *123*

Choking—Conscious Adult or Child Athlete, *125*

Cold-Related Emergencies *(see Sudden Illness—Cold-Related Emergencies, p. 167)*

Compound (or "Open") Fracture *(see Muscle, Bone and Joint [Musculoskeletal] Injuries, p. 147)*

Concussion *(see Head, Neck or Back Injury, p. 135)*

Confusion, *128*

CPR—Adult or Child *(see Checking an Unconscious Athlete—CPR, p. 109)*

Cramps *(see Muscle Injury—Cramps, p. 151 or Sudden Illness-Heat-Related Injuries, p. 172)*

Cuts *(see Wounds—Bleeding, p. 182)*

Dehydration *(see Preventing Dehydration, p. 31 and Sudden Illness-Heat-Related Emergencies, p. 171)*

Diabetic Emergency *(see Sudden Illness—Diabetic Emergency, p. 168)*

Diarrhea *(see Sudden Illness—Diarrhea, p. 169)*

Dislocation *(see Muscle, Bone and Joint [Musculoskeletal] Injuries, p. 147)*

Dizziness, *130*

Drowning (Near-Drowning), *130*

Drug Overdose *(see Substance Abuse, p. 163)*

Ear Injury *(see Wounds—Ear Injury, p. 187)*

Electrical Burn *(see Burns—Electrical, p. 99)*

Electrical Shock *(see Burns—Electrical, p. 100)*

Embedded Object *(see Wounds—Embedded Object, p. 187)*

Eye Injury *(see Wounds—Eye Injury, p. 189)*

Fainting *(see Sudden Illness—Fainting, p. 170)*

Fracture *(see Muscle, Bone and Joint (Musculoskeletal) Injuries, p. 147)*

Frostbite, *134*

Headache, *135*

Head, Neck or Back Injury, *135*

Heart Attack *(see Chest Pain or Pressure/Possible Heart Attack, p. 123)*

Heat Cramps *(see Muscle Injury—Cramps, p. 151), 139*

Heat Exhaustion *(see Sudden Illness—Heat-Related Emergencies, p. 171)*

Heat-Related Emergencies, *171*

Heat Stroke *(see Sudden Illness—Heat-Related Emergencies, p. 171)*

Heimlich Maneuver *(see Choking—Conscious Adult or Child Athlete, p. 125)*

Hives *(see Allergic Reactions, p. 72)*

Human Bite *(see Bites and Stings—Human Bite, p. 80)*

Hyperventilation *(see Breathing Emergencies—Hyperventilation, p. 93)*

Hypothermia *(see Sudden Illness—Cold-Related Emergencies, p. 167)*

Infection—Prevention, *140*

Injury *(see specific body areas injured)*, *141*

Insect Bite *(see Bites and Stings—Insect Bite, p. 81)*

Internal Injury, *141*

Itching *(see Allergic Reactions, p. 72)*

Jellyfish Sting *(see Bites and Stings—Marine Life Sting, p. 82)*

Joint Injury *(see Muscle, Bone and Joint [Musculoskeletal] Injuries, p. 147)*

Lightning Strike *(see Burns—Electrical, p. 99)*

Loss of Sensation, *143*

Lyme Disease *(see Bites and Stings—Tick Bite, p. 86)*

Mouth and Jaw Injury, *144*

Mouth to Stoma Breathing, *145*

Moving an Injured Athlete, *146*

Muscle, Bone and Joint Injuries, *147*

Muscle, Bone and Joint Injuries—Pelvic Injury, *149*

Muscle Injury—Charley Horse, *150*

Muscle Injury—Cramps, *151*

Muscle Injury—Pulled Muscle, *152*

Nausea—Sudden Illness, *153*

Nosebleed *(see Wounds—Nosebleed, p. 190)*

Paralysis *(see Loss of Sensation, p. 143)*

Pelvic Injury *(see Muscle, Bone and Joint [Musculoskeletal] Injuries—Pelvic Injury, p. 149)*

Plants—Poisonous, *154*

Poisoning, *155*

Puncture Wound *(see Wounds—Puncture, p. 191)*

Rash *(see Allergic Reactions, p. 73)*

Recovery Position *(see Checking an Unconscious Athlete—Adult or Child, p. 105)*

Rescue Breathing—Adult or Child Athlete *(see Checking an Unconscious Athlete—Rescue Breathing—Adult or Child, p. 105)*

Scorpion Sting *(see Bites and Stings—Scorpion Sting, p. 83)*

Scrapes *(see Wounds—Abrasion, p. 181)*

Seizure *(see Sudden Illness—Seizure, p. 172)*

Severed Body Part *(see Wounds—Amputation/Avulsion, p. 182)*

Shock, *158*

Smoke Inhalation, *159*
Snake Bite *(see Bites and Stings—Snake Bite, p. 84)*
Spider Bite *(see Bites and Stings—Spider Bite, p. 85)*
Spinal Injury *(see Head, Neck or Back Injury p. 135)*
Splinting (Immobilization)—*(see Muscle, Bone and Joint [Musculoskeletal] Injuries, p. 147)*
Sprains *(see Muscle, Bone and Joint [Musculoskeletal] Injuries, p. 147)*
Stingray Sting *(see Bites and Stings—Marine Life Sting, p. 82)*
Stings *(see Bites and Stings, pp. 79-88)*
Stoma *(see Mouth to Stoma Breathing, p. 108)*
Strains *(see Muscle, Bone and Joint [Musculoskeletal] Injuries, p. 147)*
Stroke *(see Sudden Illness—Stroke, p. 174)*
Substance Abuse, *163*
Sudden Illness, *165*
Sudden Illness—Cold-Related Emergencies, *167*
Sudden Illness—Diabetic Emergency, *168*
Sudden Illness—Diarrhea, *169*
Sudden Illness—Fainting, *170*
Sudden Illness—Heat Related, *171*
Sudden Illness—Seizure, *172*
Sudden Illness—Stroke, *174*
Sunburn *(see Burns—Sunburn, p. 100)*
Sweating—Unusual, *175*
Swelling, *175*
Teeth-Knocked Out, *176*
Tick Bite *(see Bites and Stings—Tick Bite, p. 86)*
Transporting an Injured Athlete, *177*
Vomiting, *178*
Wasp Sting *(see Bites and Stings—Bee Sting, p. 79)*
Water Rescue Methods *(see Drowning/Near-Drowning, p. 130)*
Wounds, *179*
Wounds—Abrasions, *180*
Wounds—Amputation/Avulsion, *182*
Wounds—Bleeding, *182*
Wounds—Bruise, *185*
Wounds—Chest Injuries, *185*

Wounds—Ear Injury, *187*
Wounds—Embedded Object, *188*
Wounds—Eye Injury, *189*
Wounds—Nosebleed, *190*
Wounds—Puncture, *191*
Wounds—Scalp Injury, *193*
5 Action Steps, *195*

The original version of this manual was developed through a combined effort of the American Red Cross and the United States Olympic Committee. Without the commitment to excellence of employees and volunteers of both organizations, this manual could not have been created.

The Health and Safety Services Sport Safety Training Development Team at American Red Cross national headquarters responsible for designing and writing the original version of this book included:

Bruce M. Carney, Project Team Leader; Rhonda Starr, Project Manager; Thomas A. Bates, EMT-B, Paul Stearns III, Associates, Educational Development; Dana N. Jessen, Manager, Program and Customer Support; Dean W. Dimke, Cathleen Reilly, Associates, Business Development and Marketing; and Jane Moore, Specialist. Administrative support was provided by Vivian Mills.

The following United States Olympic Committee staff provided guidance and review: Tom Crawford, P.E.D., Director of Coaching; Audrius Barzdukas, Associate Director of Coaching; Jan Schnittger, Manager, Coaching and Intern Programs; David Mair, Risk Manager; Sean McCann, Ph.D., Sport Psychologist; Jay T. Kearney, Ph.D., Sport Physiologist; Bob Beeten, Director, Sports Medicine; and Jenny Stone, Manager, Sports Medicine Clinical Program.

The following American Red Cross national headquarters Health and Safety Services staff provided guidance and review: Susan M. Livingstone, Vice President, Health and Safety Services; Jean Wagaman, Director, Program and Customer Support; Ferris D. Kaplan, Director, Business Development and Marketing; Earl Harbert, Manager, Contract and Financial Management; S. Elizabeth White, M.A.Ed., Manager, First Aid/CPR and Special Projects Educational Development; Karen J. Peterson, Ph.D., Senior Associate, HIV/AIDS Educational Development; Marietta Damond, Senior Associate, Program Evaluation; Martha F. Beshers, Michael Espino, Don Vardell, Associates, Educational Development; and Jennifer Deibert, Associate, Program Evaluation.

ECC Revision Team
The Sport Safety Training ECC Revision Project Team responsible for updating and revising this book included:

John Beales
Manager
Preparedness—Products
    Management & Program
    Administration
American Red Cross National
    Headquarters
Falls Church, Virginia

Betty J. Butler
Administrative Support
Preparedness—Research and
    Product Development
American Red Cross National
    Headquarters
Falls Church, Virginia

Ted T. Crites, CHES
Project Manager
Preparedness—Technical
    Development, Research and
    Product Development
American Red Cross National
    Headquarters
Falls Church, Virginia

Marc Madden
Senior Associate
Preparedness—Technical
    Development, Research and
    Product Development
American Red Cross National
    Headquarters
Falls Church, Virginia

Kyle Majchrzak
Associate
Preparedness—Products
    Management
American Red Cross National
    Headquarters
Falls Church, Virginia

Adreania McMillian
Associate
Preparedness—Technical
    Development, Research and
    Product Development
American Red Cross National
    Headquarters
Falls Church, Virginia

Heather Overstreet
Senior Associate
Communications and Marketing
American Red Cross National
    Headquarters
Washington, DC

Rick Sleutaris
Senior Associate
Preparedness—Operations
American Red Cross National
    Headquarters

Falls Church, Virginia

John Thompson
Associate
Preparedness—Products
    Management
Falls Church, Virginia

Jane Wiehe, RN
American Red Cross
Cincinnati Area Chapter
Cincinnati, Ohio

External/Chapter Reviewers

Sherri Lynn Almeida
American Red Cross National
    Advisory Council on First Aid
    and Safety
Team Health Southwest
Bellaire, Texas

Sandra Rae Badger
Cross Country/Track Coach
Intercollegiate Athletics
University of Colorado at
    Colorado Springs
Colorado Springs, Colorado

Donna Cunningham
Volunteer
Boy Scouts of America Venturing
    Division
Amarillo, Texas

Larry Cunningham
Volunteer
Boy Scouts of America Venturing
    Division
Amarillo, Texas

T. Douglas Coyle, MSHS, CHES
American Red Cross
Dallas Area Chapter
Dallas, Texas

Janice DeAngelis
Director, Health & Safety
American Red Cross
Lorain County Chapter
Elyria, Ohio.

Larry Decker
Education Specialist
American Red Cross
Pikes Peak Chapter
Colorado Springs, Colorado

Jennifer B. Hair
American Red Cross
Dallas Area Chapter
Specialist, Emergency
    Preparedness
Dallas, Texas

John Kaufmann
Supervisory Training Specialist
Naval Aviation Schools
  Command, Survival
  Department
Pensacola Naval Air Station,
  Florida

Allen Kipp
Director of Health and Safety
American Red Cross
Birmingham Area Chapter
Birmingham, Alabama

Paul R. Levins
PTI Coordinator
Naval Aviation Schools
  Command, Survival
  Department
Pensacola Naval Air Station,
  Florida

James C. O'Leary MS, ATC/L
Certified Athletic Trainer
Cleveland Clinic Sports Health
Lorain, Ohio

**Sanford (Sandy) Miller,
  ATC, LAT**
Head Athletic Trainer
Stephen F. Austin State
  University
SFA Station
Nacogodoches, Texas

Cathy Sellers
Manager, Coaching
United States Olympic
  Committee
Colorado Springs, Colorado

M. Kathryn Scott
American Red Cross National
  Advisory Council on First Aid
  and Safety
Department of Physical
  Education
University of California
Berkeley, California

Murray Stephens
USA Swimming
Meadowbrook Aquatic Center
Baltimore, Maryland

Cindy Tow, RN
American Red Cross
Birmingham Area Chapter
Birmingham, Alabama

Dave Thomas
USA Swimming
Sport Development Consultant
Southern Zone
Colorado Springs, Colorado

The StayWell editorial and production team included:

Nancy Monahan
Senior Vice President

Bill Winneberger
Senior Director of
   Manufacturing

Donna Balado
Director of Editorial

Paula Batt
Director of Sales

Reed Klanderud
Director of Marketing

Amanda Land
Marketing Manager

Jo Ann Emenecker
Editorial Project Manager

Laura O'Leary
Senior Production Manager

Louise Quinn
Publications Coordinator

■ ACKNOWLEDGMENTS

In addition to the United States Olympic Committee, the following organizations provided expert review of the materials and support for the American Red Cross Sport Safety Training Program:

VENTURING®·BSA

National Athletic
Trainers' Association

USA SWIMMING

Together We Prepare is a nationwide initiative of the American Red Cross to help everyone prepare for emergencies and disasters before they happen. Through Together We Prepare, each person is challenged to take five steps to help make their families, workplaces, schools and neighborhoods safer. The five simple steps include: make a plan, build a kit, get trained, volunteer and give blood.

This quick reference handbook is not a substitute for first aid and cardiopulmonary resuscitation (CPR)/automated external defibrillation (AED) training offered by your local Red Cross chapter but provides information related to the 'get trained' step. To learn more or to contact your local Red Cross chapter, visit the American Red Cross Web site at *www.redcross.org*

For more information on the five simple steps, see 5 Action Steps in the back of this guide.

▶ HOW TO USE THIS BOOK ◀

The *Sport Safety Training Handbook* can be used two ways:

- It is an integral part of the Sport Safety Training course. It is designed to help you learn principles of injury prevention and first aid steps for specific emergency situations.
- It is a quick source of information for either injury prevention or emergency care. Each care section guides your actions, step by step. Carry this book with you, along with your first aid kit, to every sporting event and practice.

■ ORGANIZATION

Sports injury research indicates that about half of all sports injuries could be prevented.

Part One of this book, Injury Prevention, is organized around the principles of injury prevention that apply in many sports activities, followed by descriptions of injuries common to many sports and specific prevention guidelines.

Part Two, Emergency Reference, is alphabetized so that you can find needed information easily and quickly in an emergency. For example, if someone were choking, you would find the care steps under **Choking.** Care for eye injury is described under **Eye Injury.**

To make the first aid information easy to follow, the format of the Emergency Reference section is organized to follow a pattern of **"WHAT TO LOOK FOR"** and **"WHAT TO DO"**, and in some instances includes a **"HOW TO PREVENT"** section wherever possible.

The emergency care information follows the emergency action steps described on p. xx. Always **CHECK** the scene for safety and **CHECK** the injured or ill athlete, **CALL** 9-1-1 or the local emergency number when needed, and **CARE** for the injured or ill athlete until EMS personnel arrive.

If you need information in addition to the care steps, you will be referred to related additional information. For example, when you refer to the section on **Bleeding,** that section informs you that shock is likely to occur in someone experiencing serious bleeding and refers you to the **Shock** section on p. 158.

In some cases, you may not know the nature of the athlete's injury or illness. For example, if you find an unconscious athlete on the playing field, initially you may not know where to look in the handbook for the first aid steps. In situations like this, look under what you *do* know. In this case, you know the athlete is unconscious, so start by looking under **Checking An Unconsciousness Athlete—Adult or Child,** where you will be given some appropriate care steps and be directed to other potentially helpful sections.

■ TRAINING

Training is necessary to give you the basic information you need to prevent injury and to respond effectively in an emergency. **This book is not a substitute for training!** The American Red Cross Sport Safety Training program gives you an opportunity to learn about injury prevention, practice lifesaving skills, and have questions answered by a knowledgeable instructor or referred to an appropriate resource, such as an information hotline or National Governing Body of a specific sport. Call your local American Red Cross chapter for more information on the Sport Safety Training Program.

AUTOMATED EXTERNAL DEFIBRILLATION AND THE CARDIAC CHAIN-OF-SURVIVAL

Each year approximately 250,000 people die of sudden cardiac arrest in the United States. Sudden cardiac arrest in adults is commonly caused by an abnormal heart rhythm called ventricular fibrillation (VF). This abnormal heart rhythm can also occur in young children. Disease or injury can also disrupt the heart's electrical system and damage the heart.

Defibrillation is an electric shock that interrupts the heart's chaotic electrical activity, most commonly caused by ventricular fibrillation, and can restore the heart's ability to function as a pump. An automated external defibrillator (AED) is a machine that analyzes the heart's rhythm and, if necessary, tells you to deliver a shock to a victim of sudden cardiac arrest.

The most common causes of cardiac arrest in children are:

- Airway problems;
- Breathing problems;
- Trauma or an accident (e.g., automobile, drowning, electrocution or poisoning);
- A hard blow to the chest;
- Congenital heart disease; and
- Sudden Infant Death Syndrome (SIDS)

Certain AEDs with pediatric AED pads are now capable of delivering lower levels of energy to a victim between the ages of 1 to 8 or less than 55 pounds. CPR begun immediately and continued until defibrillation is available helps to circulate blood that contains oxygen to the brain and vital organs. If the AED tells you "No shock advised," check the victim for signs of circulation. You may have to perform CPR.

The **CARDIAC CHAIN-OF-SURVIVAL** can help assure a cardiac arrest victim's best chance of survival:

1. **Early recognition and early access.** The sooner 9-1-1 or your workplace/local emergency number is called; the sooner early medical care arrives.

2. **Early CPR.** Early CPR helps circulate blood that contains oxygen to the vital organs until an AED is ready to use or advanced medical personnel arrive.
3. **Early defibrillation.** Most victims of sudden cardiac arrest need an electric shock called defibrillation. Each minute that defibrillation is delayed reduces the chance of survival by about 10 percent.
4. **Early advanced medical care.** This is given by trained medical personnel who provide further care and transport to hospital facilities.

AEDs are now deployed in greater numbers across the United States, in workplaces and places where large numbers of people gather such as at airports, shopping malls and sporting events. Acquisition, training in and use of these devices must comply with federal, state and/or local regulations and follow specific medical protocols.

◀ EMERGENCY ACTION STEPS ◀

In any emergency, always follow the same approach to caring for the injured or ill athlete. As soon as you recognize that an emergency exists, take action.

Follow these emergency action steps:
CHECK the scene for safety; check the injured or ill athlete.
CALL 9-1-1 or the local emergency number.
CARE for the athlete.

Calling for help is often the *most important* action you can take to help the athlete in need of care.

If the athlete is unconscious, call 9-1-1 or the local emergency number immediately.

Sometimes a conscious athlete will tell you not to call EMS personnel, and you may not be sure what to do. The following will assist you in determining the appropriate response.

Always **CALL** EMS personnel if the injured athlete—

- Is or becomes unconscious.
- Is confused.
- Has breathing difficulty.
- Is not breathing or has no pulse.
- Has persistent chest pain or pressure.
- Is bleeding severely.
- Has pressure or pain in the abdomen that does not go away.
- Is vomiting or passing blood in the urine or feces.
- Has a seizure, severe headache, or slurred speech.
- Appears to have been poisoned.
- Has injuries to the head, neck, or back.
- Has possible broken bones.
- Has severe burns.

Also **CALL** 9-1-1 or the local emergency number for any of these situations:

- Fire or explosion
- Swiftly moving or rapidly rising water
- Presence of poisonous gas
- Vehicle collisions
- Athletes who cannot be moved easily

FIRST AID KIT

Be prepared for an emergency. Keep a first aid kit nearby during all coaching and sporting activities. Whenever possible, have a second kit for multiple injury situations at a practice or competition site.

A sports first aid kit used in athletics should include:

- Adhesive bandages with gauze pads—assorted sizes;
- Alcohol/alcohol preps;
- Alcohol-based hand rubs;
- Antibacterial ointment;
- Anti-infective solution such as hydrogen peroxide;

- Antiseptic towelettes;
- Arm sling (triangular bandage is fine);
- Bandage scissors;
- Biohazard bag;
- Butterfly closures—1/8" X 3";
- Cold packs;
- Cotton swabs;
- CPR breathing barrier;
- Elastic tape—2";
- Elastic wraps—2", 4"and 6";
- Emergency blanket;
- Eye patch;
- Eye wash;
- Flashlight and batteries;
- Foam padding, assorted thicknesses;
- Gloves, disposable (such as latex or non-latex; several pairs);
- List of emergency phone numbers;
- Moleskin;
- Nail clippers;
- Nonstick wound dressing pads—3" X 4";
- Petroleum jelly;
- Plastic bags for ice;
- Powder;
- Protective eyewear;
- Roller gauze;
- Safety pins;
- Splinting materials;
- *Sport Safety Training Handbook*;
- Sterile gauze pads—3" X 4" or 4" X 4";
- Sunscreen;
- Tape adherent;
- Tape remover;
- Tape underwrap;
- Thermometer (non-mercury/non-glass);

- Tongue blades;
- Tweezers; and
- White tape—1" and 1 1/2".

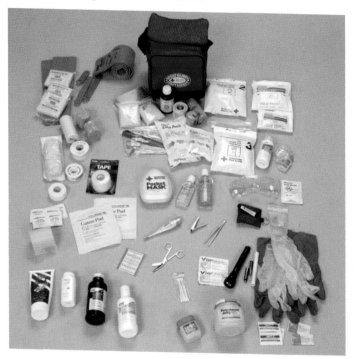

Whether you buy a first aid kit or put one together, be certain that all the items previously listed are included. Check the kit regularly to make sure flashlight batteries still work and that it contains all the necessary supplies. Replace any items that have expired or been used. Depending on your facility, you may want to include walkie-talkies, a cell phone or coins for phone calls. Other unique items may be necessary depending on the sport such as face-mask removal tools (you should be thoroughly familiar with their use).

INJURY PREVENTION

PART ONE

■ COACHING RESPONSIBILITIES

Responsible coaching is a major factor in reducing injuries. Coaches should follow these general guidelines:

1. Remember what motivates athletes, particularly children, to play their sport. Their goal is seldom just to win or excel. Young athletes give the following as their primary reasons for being involved in athletics:
   - Have fun, enjoy excitement of competition
   - Improve skills, face challenges, learn new skills
   - Get exercise, stay in shape
   - Enjoy teamwork
2. Know the rules of the sport and insist your athletes also know and follow them. Teach your athletes to play fair. Conduct training and competition within the rules.
3. Understand the basics of skill development and training methods appropriate for the level of your athletes. Learn and stay informed about coaching based on the principles of growth and development.
4. Follow the safety guidelines of your sport's NGB.
5. Teach sportsmanship by example; make sure players feel good about doing their best, regardless of winning or losing. Never ridicule or shout at players for making mistakes or for losing.
6. Balance constructive criticism with support and praise.
7. Ensure that equipment and the facility are safe.
8. Educate athletes about the dangers of nutritional and substance abuse.

■ PRESEASON MEDICAL EXAMINATION

A preseason medical examination is a comprehensive medical evaluation performed by a qualified physician prior to any participation in a sport to determine an athlete's ability to train and compete.

Coaches and administrators should note that there are two types of preseason medical evaluations. The general physical evaluation is used by many scholastic or recreational programs in which athletes participate in several sports or only on a limited basis. The specialized medical evaluation is for athletes who compete at higher levels, which involves a more advanced and detailed screening.

A general medical evaluation should be thorough and focus on broad health issues, including reviews of past problems and conditions related to family medical histories. The more specific medical evaluation should include an examination of specific performance-related skills and the athlete's medical capability to perform them, such as strength and flexibility tests and tightness in highly used muscle groups.

IMPORTANCE FOR ATHLETES

An appropriate medical examination helps assess overall health, reveal past and present injuries that might be aggravated by participation in the sport and identify conditions that could result in injuries. When preexisting conditions or injuries are found, treatment can be prescribed to heal the injury or alleviate the condition before training begins.

GUIDELINES FOR THE MEDICAL APPROVAL/EXAMINATION

1. Athletes should schedule examinations 4 to 6 weeks before the first practice so that any current injuries or physical problems can be addressed and, if needed, to permit referrals to specialists.

2. Suggest that athletes be examined by a physician or health care provider who is familiar with their medical history. It is desirable to use a physician who is familiar with sports medicine.

3. The examining physician should know in which sport the athletes will be participating.

4. The medical examination should include a thorough and up-to-date medical history that addresses:
   - Previous injuries;
   - Allergies;
   - Medications;
   - Hospitalizations;
   - Operations;
   - Immunizations;
   - Family heart conditions;
   - Skin conditions;
   - Cold or heat sensitivities;
   - Dietary habits;
   - Eating disorders;
   - Real or perceived weight problems; and
   - Use of anabolic steroids and other drugs.

5. The medical examinations should evaluate:
   - General cardiovascular, musculoskeletal, and nutritional health;
   - Fitness for the specific sport;
   - Existing injuries;
   - Conditions that might result in injuries; and
   - Conditions that might limit or prevent participation in specific sports.

6. Physicians should discuss with the athletes the completed evaluation, any unsafe practices (e.g., drug use), and dietary guidelines.
7. Written notification of any problems or special conditions should be provided to the coaches.
8. Medical examinations should meet all legal and insurance requirements.
9. The physician should state in writing that there are no medical reasons to limit, restrict, or prohibit the athlete from participating.
10. All medical information is *confidential* and should be kept private. It should not be disclosed to anyone who does not have a medical need to know.

■ EMERGENCY ACTION PLAN

An Emergency Action Plan is a written plan that every program and facility should have to prepare for potential emergencies. Certain types of emergencies, such as specific natural disasters, are more likely in some locations than in others. Emergencies, however, can occur anywhere. In addition to injuries, emergencies may include illnesses, such as heart attack, seizure or stroke. Emergencies can result from a specific problem, such as fire, power failure, chemical spills, violent winds, tornadoes, lightning, earthquake, mudslides or sudden flooding.

The facility's Emergency Action Plan should address all relevant categories of emergencies. It should be practiced and reviewed on a regular basis to ensure the effectiveness of the plan. Such plans should define the responsibility of everyone who may be involved, covering areas such as the following.

▶*Content of an Emergency Action Plan*
- Layout
  - EMS personnel access and entry/exit routes
  - Location of rescue and first aid equipment, including AEDs

- Location of telephones, with emergency telephone numbers posted
- Location of keys to reach telephones or equipment
- Exits and evacuation routes
- Equipment
  - Rescue equipment
  - First aid supplies
  - Emergency equipment (flashlights, fire extinguisher, etc.)
- Support Personnel
  - Within facility
  - Coaches
  - Athletic trainers
  - Athletic officials and referees
  - Facility administrators
  - Management personnel
  - Teachers
  - School nurse/physician
  - Athletic director
  - Clerical personnel
  - Maintenance personnel
- External (provide telephone numbers)
  - EMS personnel
  - Police
  - Fire
  - Hazardous materials (Hazmat) team
  - Poison Control Center
  - Hospitals
  - Power and gas companies
  - Health department
- Staff Responsibilities
  - Assign each staff member a duty:
  - Person(s) to provide care
  - Person(s) to control bystanders and supervise other athletes
  - Person(s) to meet EMS personnel

- Person(s) to transport injured athlete when appropriate
- Communication
  - When and how to call 9-1-1 or the local emergency number (such as how to access an outside phone line)
  - Chain of command
  - Person to contact family/guardian
  - Person to deal with media
- Follow-up
  - Complete appropriate documentation (incident report, accident report, etc.)
  - Replace equipment and supplies
  - Emergency Action Plan evaluation
  - Staff debriefing
  - Critical Incident Stress Debriefing (if necessary)
  - Check on condition of injured athlete

■ CHECKING THE FACILITY AREA

Although facility managers, school departments and other building owners and operators have certain responsibilities for providing a safe environment for training and competing, coaches are responsible for ensuring that locker rooms, workout rooms, gymnasiums, equipment, fields, bleachers and courses are safe. Coaches also should ensure that proper emergency care and safety equipment is available and accessible.

IMPORTANCE FOR ATHLETES

A safe environment for training and competing can considerably reduce the incidence of athletic injuries.

GUIDELINES TO PROVIDE A SAFE ENVIRONMENT

1. Regularly and thoroughly inspect all building areas, drinking fountains, pools, equipment, fields, bleachers, courses and other playing surfaces used by your athletes.
2. Inspect potentially dangerous equipment (e.g., ropes, guide lines, trampolines, diving boards, jumping pits and pads), heavy-use equipment (e.g., playing surfaces, sleds, watercraft), and protective equipment (e.g., helmets, pads, guards) much more frequently.
3. Ensure that unused equipment is not stored in or dangerously close to a playing area.
4. Ensure that wall-mounted devices that could cause injury are padded and light bulbs have protective coverings.
5. During extreme weather (e.g., rain, high wind, ice), inspect equipment and fields, courses, and other outside playing surfaces, including support structures (e.g., tents, trailers), that could become unsafe.
6. Work with athletes to develop responsibility and respect for equipment.
7. Ask athletes to report any unsafe conditions related to the facility, pools, equipment, fields, courses and other playing surfaces.
8. Know the maintenance techniques and schedules for the facility, pool, fields, bleachers, courses and other playing surfaces, and make sure they are enforced.
9. Report in writing damage to the facility, pools, fields, bleachers and courses, and request to have it repaired. Inspect repairs when completed. Keep a record of all such requests.

10. Know the maintenance/replacement techniques and schedules for equipment.
11. Report in writing serious damage to equipment, and make sure that worn, damaged or broken equipment is repaired, replaced or not used.
12. Prevent athletes from using unsafe building areas, pools, equipment, fields, courses and other playing surfaces. In particular, remove unsafe equipment immediately to prevent inadvertent or prohibited use.
13. Ensure adequate fluid replacement for athletes during all practices and competitions.
14. Ensure easy access to emergency equipment and first aid supplies by clearly marking the location of First Aid Kits and AED equipment (if available).
15. Ensure telephone or radio access to enable contact with emergency medical services.

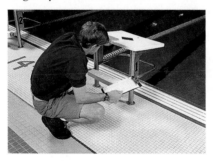

■ EQUIPMENT SELECTION AND USE

The coach is responsible for determining what equipment will be used in training and competing, regardless of the supplier, selecting appropriate equipment, making sure that equipment is available, overseeing the use of equipment and ensuring that equipment is properly maintained and replaced when needed. Never modify equipment without consulting with and obtaining written agreement from the manufacturer. Any modifications to equipment may void equipment warranties and create liability concerns.

IMPORTANCE FOR ATHLETES

Proper equipment can protect athletes from injury or reduce the severity of injury if one occurs, as well as enhance performance. To maximize injury prevention, equipment must be:

- Consistently used;
- Available;
- Appropriate;
- High-quality;
- In good condition;
- Sized properly;
- Fitted correctly;
- Maintained; and
- Repaired or replaced when damaged.

GUIDELINES FOR EQUIPMENT SELECTION AND USE

1. Be knowledgeable about the different types of equipment available, including new developments in equipment materials and design.
2. Deal only with reputable suppliers and authorized dealers.
3. Provide quality equipment that is appropriate for the sport and size, strength and skill level of the user.
4. Ensure athletes' safety by requiring the use of helmets, eye protection, mouth guards and other critical safety equipment where appropriate.
5. Ensure that equipment meets all required codes or standards.
6. Understand equipment liability and misuse.
7. Have enough equipment on hand so that every athlete has access to appropriate equipment.
8. Inspect all new equipment for quality and defects before use.

9. Inspect all equipment—both that belonging to the athlete and that provided to the athlete—for wear at the beginning of each season. Be cautious of hand-me-down equipment.
10. During the season, inspect equipment periodically for wear and damage.
11. Know how to size equipment. Always follow manufacturers' recommendations.
12. Instruct athletes on the proper use, fit, cleaning and maintenance of equipment.
13. Warn athletes about any dangers associated with equipment use.
14. Establish clear rules for equipment use and care and penalties for misuse.
15. Ensure proper care and use of equipment.
16. Establish a schedule for cleaning and maintaining equipment, especially shared equipment (e.g., batting helmets).
17. Have equipment repaired or replaced when needed.
18. Instruct athletes to report equipment damage.
19. Direct athletes to repair or replace their personal equipment when necessary.
20. Do not allow athletes to use unsafe equipment.
21. Maintain proper documentation regarding inventory, assignments to athletes and inspections and maintenance of equipment.

■ SUPERVISING ATHLETES

Coaches are responsible for providing appropriate supervision to prevent unnecessary risk of injury. Coaches use two types of supervision. General supervision is the oversight of all areas and events taking place during the session, whether training or competition. Specific supervision is the oversight of specific elements or skills being performed.

For the coach, this balance is important for protecting the health of athletes, because as the level of specific supervision increases (often targeted at a single athlete), the level of general supervision often decreases. The coach must continue to be aware of the activities of all athletes present.

GUIDELINES FOR APPROPRIATE SUPERVISION

A coach's supervision responsibilities start when the **first** athlete arrives at the sport facility and do not end until the **last** athlete leaves. Make sure that the drop off and pick up areas are safe.

1. Consider athletes' maturity, age, size, weight, conditioning and skill when determining the degree of supervision required.
2. Supervise athletes in all activities related to the sport:
   - Traveling to and from training and competition, when appropriate
   - Staying overnight
   - Eating meals
   - Dressing, assembling equipment, and otherwise preparing for training and competition
   - Warming up
   - Training and competing
   - Cooling down
   - Putting equipment away, showering, and otherwise concluding training and competition
   - Receiving treatment for injuries

3. Act quickly and decisively to correct conditions and actions that could lead to injury or damage.
4. Properly plan and direct activities.
5. Increase the level of specific supervision as the risk of injury increases.
6. Insist that athletes use appropriate training techniques.
7. Ensure that athletes use equipment safely.
8. Make sure that athletes use facilities, fields and courses safely.
9. Be alert to conditions that require additional supervision.
10. Be alert to changing conditions that could increase the risk of injury.
11. Increase the level of supervision when athletes are learning new techniques or using equipment.
12. Do not delegate authority unless you are positive that discipline and control will be maintained.
13. Be accessible to athletes and other coaches.
14. Be sensitive to an athlete's feelings and dignity if an embarrassing situation occurs as a result of an injury or illness.

GUIDELINES FOR PARENTS

If parents are involved in your sports activities, parental action or inaction can play a significant role in preventing or lessening the severity of injuries. Coaches must clearly and firmly communicate to parents how they can help or inadvertently harm athletes and what the parents' role should be.

IMPORTANCE FOR ATHLETES

Supportive parents can assist athletes in their training and competition, as well as help them maintain their psychological fitness.

GUIDELINES FOR WORKING EFFECTIVELY WITH PARENTS

1. Develop an understanding and supportive working relationship with parents, families and guardians.
2. At the beginning of each season, clearly communicate the following either with a face-to-face parent orientation or by distributing a fact sheet containing:
   - Medical requirements (e.g., the preseason medical examination);
   - What the sport entails (for younger athletes);
   - The physical demands on the athletes;
   - The psychological demands on the athletes;
   - The potential for injury;
   - Your coaching philosophy and methods;
   - Your goals for the season;
   - The importance or lack of importance of winning/losing;
   - The need to learn from mistakes;
   - How athletes are chosen to participate;
   - The vast differences in athletes' developmental and skill levels;
   - The fact that boys and girls will be competing together (if applicable);
   - The training schedule-formal practice and practice at home (if applicable);
   - The schedule of competitive events;
   - The equipment requirements, cost, and where to get it;
   - The nutritional requirements;
   - The dangers and signals of nutritional abuse and eating disorders (see *p. 32*);
   - The need for support, but not pressure;
   - The dangers of competitive stress;

- The importance of rest;
- The guidelines for parent behavior during competition (*see # 5 below*); and
- How to contact you.

3. Encourage parents, family members, and agents to talk with you about any of their questions or concerns.
4. As appropriate, involve parents as assistant coaches, equipment managers, drivers, phone-chain managers, etc.
5. Specify acceptable parental behavior at competitive events, such as:
   - Staying in the spectator area;
   - Remaining seated (if applicable);
   - Not coaching from the sidelines;
   - Not making derogatory comments about any athletes, parents or officials; and
   - Not advising, criticizing or otherwise interfering with the coach.
6. Direct parents, family members and agents to closely monitor athletes' medical needs and report any concerns, particularly:
   - Overexertion;
   - Overuse; and
   - Stress.

■ PREVENTING FURTHER INJURY

When injuries occur, coaches must act quickly and decisively to prevent further injury.

IMPORTANCE FOR ATHLETES

Correcting unsafe conditions helps provide a safe environment for training and competing.

GUIDELINES FOR PREVENTING FURTHER INJURY

1. Review programs and survey the environment to identify the cause or causes of injuries and take corrective actions.
2. Establish a written record of the corrective actions taken.
3. When appropriate, review the injury, the causes and the corrective actions with your athletes and other members of the coaching staff.

■ INJURY PREVENTION CHECKLIST

Ensure that all the following safety steps have been taken before the season begins, during training and competition, and after the season ends.

▶ *Before the Season*

___ Update policies and regulations
___ Medical examination/approval
___ Parental permission forms signed
___ Time and location of practices
___ Team/group matching (size, weight and skill level)
___ Preseason conditioning
___ Training program preparation
    ___ Staff skill training
    ___ Instructional materials
    ___ Practice plans
___ Emergency Action Plans
___ First aid kit stocked and available
___ Emergency numbers
___ *Sport Safety Training Handbook*
___ All coaches properly trained and certified
___ Proper orientations arranged for new coaches
___ Facility inspection
___ Equipment inspection
___ Communication equipment available, with backup system available

___ Parent orientation program (if applicable)
___ Athlete orientation
    ___ Risks
    ___ Safety procedures
    ___ Injury prevention
    ___ Changes in rules, techniques or equipment
    ___ Equipment use and maintenance instruction
    ___ Facility use instructions
    ___ Documentation that athletes have been oriented

▶ During Training and Competition

___ Training program assessment and revision
___ General supervision
___ Program implementation
___ Equipment use
___ Environment (heat, cold, hazardous weather)
___ Periodic facility inspection and maintenance (document dates and results)
___ Periodic equipment inspection and maintenance (document dates and results)

▶ After the Season

___ Off-season conditioning
___ Program assessment and revision
___ Staff skill training assessment
___ Injury cause and response evaluation
___ Facility inspection
___ Equipment inspection

▶ PREVENTING SPECIFIC INJURIES ◀

■ HEAD, NECK AND BACK INJURIES

Follow all injury prevention guidelines to help prevent head, neck and back injury. Should an injury involve the head or spine, recognize the potential for serious injury and respond to prevent further injury to the spinal cord (*see Head, Neck or Back Injury in Part 2, p. 135*).

A concussion is a temporary impairment of brain function caused by a blow to the head. The primary signals are momentary loss of consciousness and memory loss or confusion. The primary goal of care is to determine whether emergency medical care is needed for a serious condition and to call EMS personnel when appropriate.

■ RECOGNIZING SPINAL INJURY

The way an injury occurred may give you some idea if a spinal injury is likely. The following are situations in which a spinal injury is possible:

- Any fall from higher than the person's height
- Any athlete found unconscious for an unknown reason
- Any significant head injury, especially with contact at the crown or forehead
- Any injury related to a diving board, water slide or diving from a height (such as a bank or a cliff)
- Any dive into shallow water
- Any violent collision

In addition, look for the following signals of a possible head, neck or back injury:

- Severe pain or pressure in the head, neck or back
- Tingling or lack of sensation in the extremities
- Partial or complete loss of movement of any body part
- Unusual bumps or depressions on the head or neck
- Sudden memory loss
- Change in level of consciousness
- Persistent headache
- Blood or other fluids in the ears or nose
- Heavy external bleeding of the head, neck or back
- Seizures
- Impaired speaking, vision or breathing as a result of the injury

- Nausea or vomiting
- Loss of balance
- Bruising of the head, especially around the eyes or behind the ears

GUIDELINES TO PREVENT SPINAL INJURY

1. Do not move the athlete unless absolutely necessary.
2. Support the head and neck in the position in which the athlete was found.
3. Call 9-1-1 or the local emergency number and wait for EMS personnel to arrive.
4. If CPR is necessary, minimize movement of the head and neck by opening the airway with the jaw thrust maneuver. (*see Checking an Unconscious Athlete—Adult or Child, p. 103*).
5. Provide additional care for the injury (*see Head, Neck or Back Injury, p. 135*).

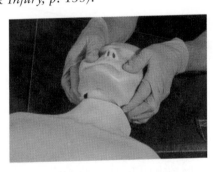

MUSCLE, BONE AND JOINT (MUSCULOSKELETAL) INJURIES

■ WARM-UP/COOL-DOWN

Warm-up activities, stretching exercises, calisthenics and slowly increasing the intensity of motion—prepare the body for training and competition, both physiologically and psychologically. Likewise, cool-down activities—light activity and slow, sustained stretching-help the body make the transition from vigorous activity to a normal state of activity.

IMPORTANCE FOR ATHLETES

Warm-Up:

Beginning a training session or competition without warming up greatly increases the chance of injury. A proper warm-up helps athletes train and compete without being injured by:

- Increasing the body temperature;
- Increasing the rate of respiration (oxygen availability);
- Increasing the heart rate;
- Reducing the risk of muscle and tendon strains by stretching tight muscles; and
- Reducing the risk of ligament sprains.

Cool-Down:

Blood and muscle lactic acid levels drop faster during active cool-down than during rest. Abruptly stopping intensive physical activity can result in muscle cramps, soreness and stiffness and may increase the potential for fainting or dizziness caused by blood pooling. A proper cool-down enhances athletic activity by:

- Gradually reducing muscle workout intensity;
- Continuing the muscle-pump action to allow increased blood circulation;
- Reducing pooling of blood; and
- Helping remove wastes.

GUIDELINES FOR WARM-UP/COOL-DOWN ACTIVITIES

Warm-Up:
1. Inform athletes of the importance of properly warming up.
2. Teach athletes the warm-up activities to perform before training and competing.
   - First, perform an appropriate activity (for strength) depending on the sport to raise the body temperature.
   - Second, perform an appropriate stretching exercise for flexibility.
   - Third, perform partial- and full-motion activities for each athlete's particular position or event, at varying speeds, distances or intensities.
3. Direct warm-up activities of athletes to ensure a slow increase in the intensity of motion, particularly the motion actually used in the sport.
4. Ensure that warm-up activities are tailored to each athlete's conditioning and position or event.
5. Ensure that athletes warm up for at least 10 minutes.
6. Ensure that warm-up activities do not cause fatigue.

Cool-Down:
1. Inform athletes of the importance of properly cooling down the body after exercise.
2. Teach athletes the cool-down activities to perform after training and competing.
   - First, perform partial- and full-motion activities for each athlete's particular position/event, at reduced speeds, distances or intensities.

- Second, perform light calisthenics.
- Third, perform stretching exercises.
3. Direct cool-down activities to ensure a gradual reduction of the intensity of activity.
4. Ensure that athletes perform the cool-down activity for at least 10 minutes.

■ TRAINING METHODS

Training methods and the type, frequency, duration and intensity of training should vary among athletes, depending on the athlete's age, physical conditioning, mental state, sport played and training goals. The purpose of training is to prepare for competition. Training is not disciplinary activity, unsupervised play or competition itself.

IMPORTANCE FOR ATHLETES

In addition to improving performance, appropriate training is an important element of injury prevention in all sports. Training that focuses on correct technique can help prevent both chronic and overuse injury.

GUIDELINES FOR TRAINING

1. Ensure that training begins before the season starts so that athletes are in good condition for the first day

of practice. Injuries are more likely when poorly conditioned athletes overtrain early in the season.

2. Ensure that training balances fitness and skill development in all training sessions.
3. Require proper warm-up (*see Warm-Up/ Cool-Down, p. 21*).
4. Ensure that training intensity increases gradually. Trying to progress too rapidly often leads to injury.
5. Increase training time, distance or repetitions no more than 10 percent weekly.
6. Recognize the impact of cumulative training increases, such as simultaneous increases in duration, frequency and intensity.
7. Teach athletes to be aware of their training levels.
8. Note athletes' changes in skill levels and techniques.
9. Encourage variation in athletic activities.
10. Use strength and weight training when appropriate, but only with proper instruction and supervision.
11. In warmer, more humid climates, modify training to prevent heat-related emergencies (*see Heat-Related Emergencies, p. 171*).
12. Require proper cool-down (*see Warm-Up/Cool-Down, p. 21*).

■ PREVENTING OVERUSE INJURIES

Overuse injuries—such as bursitis, shin splints, stress fractures and tendonitis—generally are caused by repetitive stress and damage to tissue.

Overuse injuries generally occur more often in organized sports, as opposed to acute sports injuries, which occur in both play and organized activities. Primary contributing factors to overuse injuries include the following:

● Athletes in organized sports often overtrain or continue to participate when fatigued or injured;

- Coaches—most often volunteer amateurs coaching in youth programs—may be unaware of appropriate conditioning, training, and techniques;
- Athletes often fail to report injuries;
- Coaches fail to recognize the signals of overuse injuries;
- Young athletes are predisposed to overuse injuries because of the physiology of growing;
- The growth cartilage of younger athletes is more easily damaged than the cartilage in older athletes;
- Muscles and tendons of younger athletes tend to be tighter than in older athletes because of rapid bone growth;
- Young athletes specialize in a select sport or sports at too early an age; and
- Athletes sometimes avoid sports with a high risk of acute injury (e.g., rugby) without properly understanding that overuse injuries can occur in seemingly safe sports (e.g., swimming).

IMPORTANCE FOR ATHLETES

Severe overuse injuries can impact future sports participation and physical activities of any athlete. In general, young athletes are more susceptible to overuse injuries than older athletes, and these injuries to young athletes may have more serious long-term consequences than to older athletes. Fortunately, most overuse injuries can be prevented.

Risk factors for overuse injuries include:
- Growth (younger athletes);
- Musculoskeletal weakness;
- Malnutrition;
- Obesity;
- Rapid increases in training frequency, duration or intensity;

- Strength imbalances;
- Flexibility imbalances;
- Misalignment of legs;
- Improper or ill-fitting footwear;
- Hard playing surface;
- Past injuries; and
- Inadequate rest or fatigue.

Stages of overuse injuries:
- Initially, pain occurs only after the activity.
- Eventually, pain begins to occur during and after the activity.
- Later, pain occurs throughout the activity.
- Finally, pain occurs during sport and nonsport activities.

GUIDELINES TO PREVENT OVERUSE INJURIES

1. Know the risk factors.
2. Improve training in proper technique for coaches, particularly amateur coaches.
3. Require sport-specific pre-participation physical examinations.
4. Develop fitness by increasing strength, flexibility and endurance.
5. Encourage athletes to report pain and injuries.
6. Positively respond to athletes' complaints of pain.
7. Inform parents about general risk factors, sport-specific stress areas and the signals of overuse injuries.
8. Increase training time, distance and repetitions no more than 10 percent a week.

OTHER EMERGENCIES

■ PREVENTING HEAT-RELATED EMERGENCIES

Heat-related emergencies, or hyperthermia, may be life threatening. Heat stroke, heat exhaustion and heat cramps result from the body losing so much fluid that its natural cooling mechanism fails and the body overheats. Conditions contributing to heat-related emergencies include:

- Hot environmental conditions;
- High humidity;
- Extreme physical exertion;
- Inappropriately layered or rubberized clothing; and
- Inadequate fluid intake.

IMPORTANCE FOR ATHLETES

Heat-related emergencies may result in illness, shock and even death. Fortunately, heat-related emergencies are preventable.

In general, younger athletes are more susceptible to heat-related emergencies than older athletes because:

- Children do not cool naturally in hot weather as effectively as adults;
- Children are slower to adjust to hot conditions than adults; and
- Children often do not instinctively replenish fluids.

GUIDELINES TO PREVENT HEAT-RELATED EMERGENCIES

1. Schedule practice during cooler times of the day.
2. Use appropriate equipment. When appropriate, instruct athletes to:
   - Wear net-type jerseys;
   - Wear light-weight, light-colored, cotton T-shirts and shorts;
   - Remove helmets and pads (if applicable) when not playing/scrimmaging;
   - Avoid wearing sweat suits; and
   - Change sweat-soaked clothing.
3. Be certain athletes are fully hydrated before practice and competition.

4. Schedule and enforce frequent water breaks.
5. Do not use salt tablets.
6. Reduce or cancel practice when the weather is excessively hot or humid.
7. When athletes are practicing or competing, allow time for adjustment to warmer climates.

■ PREVENTING COLD-RELATED EMERGENCIES

Cold-related emergencies include hypothermia and frostbite. Hypothermia is a condition in which the body's warming mechanisms cannot maintain normal core body temperature and the body cools. Contributing factors for body cooling include air temperature, humidity, wind and the condition of the skin (wet or dry). Frostbite is the freezing of local skin or body areas. Hypothermia and frostbite may occur together or separately.

IMPORTANCE FOR ATHLETES

Outdoor sports in cool or cold weather, particularly those in or around snow, ice or water, place athletes at risk for frostbite or hypothermia. Hypothermia is generally caused by prolonged exposure to wet, windy and cold environments. Frostbite may occur as a result of being underdressed for the weather conditions or simply remaining in the cold too long without adequate protection.

Hypothermia may be a life-threatening medical emergency. Frostbite may result in disability or loss of body tissue.

GUIDELINES TO PREVENT HYPOTHERMIA

1. **Do not** start an activity in, on or around cold water unless you know you can get help quickly in an emergency.
2. Be aware of the wind chill.

3. Dress appropriately and avoid staying in the cold too long.
4. Drink plenty of warm fluids or warm water.
5. Avoid caffeine and alcohol.
6. Stay active to maintain body heat.
7. Take frequent breaks from the cold.
8. Wear a Coast Guard-approved life jacket (Personal Floatation Device [PFD]) while boating. Have life jackets on hand whenever you are near cold water. A life jacket will help you float in a rescue position if you fall into cold water, and some styles provide insulation against cold water.
9. If you are near water in cold weather, wear rain gear or wool clothes. Wool insulates you even when it is wet. Wear layers of clothing and wear a hat. As much as 60 percent of body heat loss occurs through the head.
10. Carry matches in a waterproof container. You may need to build a fire to warm up after a fall into cold water.
11. Carry a high-energy food containing sugar. Sugar stimulates shivering, the body's internal mechanism for rewarming itself.

GUIDELINES TO PREVENT FROSTBITE

1. Dress appropriately and avoid staying in the cold too long. Wear a hat and gloves when appropriate with layers of clothing.
2. Avoid unnecessary exposure of any part of the body to the cold.
3. Drink plenty of warm fluids or warm water.
4. Avoid caffeine and alcohol.
5. Take frequent breaks from the cold.
6. Get out of the cold immediately if the signals of frostbite appear: skin that appears waxy, is cold to the

touch or is discolored (flushed, white, yellow, blue). Give care (p. 134).

■ PREVENTING WEATHER-RELATED INJURIES

Weather conditions may affect the safety of athletes in all outdoor and some indoor activities. Because weather conditions vary greatly in different parts of the United States, you should know the conditions of which to be aware of at your facility and follow your facility's weather-related guidelines.

Lightning strikes the ground in the United States millions of times each year causing about a hundred deaths and hundreds more injuries. People who are active outdoors need to be aware of the potential danger and be prepared to take quick actions to avoid injury.

IMPORTANCE FOR ATHLETES

Weather-related injuries include being struck by lightning or being injured by hail or debris from high winds, tornadoes or other storm conditions. *Lightning strikes are one of the leading causes of death for children under age 10 in organized sports.* These injuries can easily be prevented. Take weather conditions seriously.

GUIDELINES TO PREVENT WEATHER-RELATED INJURIES

1. Pay attention to weather forecasts, and monitor weather reports, particularly with changing weather patterns.
2. If possible, find shelter in a substantial building or in a fully enclosed (metal) vehicle such as an automobile, truck or a van with the windows completely closed.

3. Designate someone to watch for and notify sports officials or referees of changes in weather.

4. If far from a weatherproof shelter, watch cloud patterns and conditions for signals of an approaching storm.

5. Designate safe locations and move or evacuate athletes to a safe location at the first sound of thunder. Every 5 seconds between the flash of lightning and the sound (bang) of thunder equals 1 mile of distance.

6. In a storm, keep everyone away from windows. Injuries may occur from flying debris or glass if the window breaks.

7. Do not let anyone shower during a thunderstorm. Water and metal are both excellent conductors of electricity.

8. Do not use a telephone, cell phone or radio transmitter except for emergencies.

9. If caught outdoors and there is not enough time to reach a safe building:
   - Keep away from structures in open areas, such as picnic shelters and dugouts;
   - Keep away from tall, isolated trees or objects that project above the landscape;
   - Keep away from water and grounded objects, such as metal fences, metal bleachers, tanks, rails and pipes;
   - Avoid the high ground; and
   - If caught out in the open and lightning is striking nearby, minimize contact with the ground and crouch down with feet together. Cover your ears with your hands to avoid hearing damage from the thunder.

10. If there is a tornado alert, go to the location specified in the facility's Emergency Action Plan. This may be the basement or the lowest interior level of a building.

11. Wait at least 30 minutes after thunder and lightning stop entirely before allowing athletes to return outdoors. Continue to watch for approaching storms and monitor weather forecasts.
12. In indoor facilities, changes in outdoor conditions, particularly those that are unseasonable, may affect facility conditions (e.g., warmer temperatures and increased humidity). Be aware of these situations because athletes accustomed to a cooler indoor temperature may sweat more, resulting in a less secure grip on equipment or more perspiration on floor surfaces.

■ PREVENTING DEHYDRATION

Dehydration occurs when athletes fail to drink enough liquids to replace fluids lost through perspiration or urine output. Other causes include:

- Infection or illness;
- Profuse sweating;
- Reduced electrolyte intake, such as potassium found in some foods (e.g., fruit) and fluids;
- Injection of hypertonic solutions, such as intravenous solutions while under medical care; and
- Ingestion of diuretic substances (e.g., salt, caffeine).

IMPORTANCE FOR ATHLETES

Dehydrated athletes do not perform well. Fluid loss through sweating directly impacts strength, endurance, power and cognitive abilities. Excessive fluid loss may cause an athlete to feel fatigued, weak, irritable, nauseous, dizzy and even disoriented.

GUIDELINES TO PREVENT DEHYDRATION

1. 2 to 3 hours before a workout or competition: Have athlete drink 2 cups of fluid.

2. One hour before a workout or competition: Have athlete drink 1 cup of fluid.
3. Fifteen minutes before a workout or competition: Have athlete drink 1/2 cup of fluid.
4. Before a workout or competition: Weigh each athlete.
5. Every 10 to 20 minutes during a workout or competition: Have athlete drink 1/2 cup of fluid.
6. After a workout or competition: Weigh each athlete and have athlete drink 2 cups of fluid for every pound of weight lost.

GUIDELINES FOR REHYDRATION

1. Athlete should drink cool fluids, such as water.
2. Athlete should drink Four 8-ounce glasses of fluid for every 1000 calories expended.

■ PREVENTING NUTRITIONAL ABUSE AND EATING DISORDERS

Nutritional abuse and eating disorders are a significant problem in sports. They include:

● **Anorexia nervosa—**
  • An intense fear of becoming fat that tends to increase with weight loss. Refusal to maintain normal weight. Most often affects teenage women but has

also occurred in male athletes; Also related to extreme dieting by athletes trying to "make weight."

- **Bulimia—**
  - A neurotic disorder characterized by heavy overeating followed by forced vomiting, fasting or induced diarrhea. Most often occurs in adolescents and young-adult women.
- **Eating to bulk—**
  - Eating simply to add weight, often without proper physical training.
- **Poor nutrition—**
  - Eating improper foods due to poor eating habits, ignorance of good nutrition or poverty.
- **Compulsive overeating—**
  - Obsessive with food; consuming large amounts of junk food.

Anorexia and bulimia are true psychological illnesses with physical symptoms and must be treated by professional personnel, including psychologists, physicians, and nutritionists.

IMPORTANCE FOR ATHLETES

Proper nutrition and normal eating habits are extremely important for athletes' ability to train and compete, as well as for athletes' general health, resistance to and recovery from injury and illness, normal growth and development and long-term well-being. Importantly, nutritional abuse and eating disorders may be signals of emotional problems, such as those related to competitive stress, self-image and self-esteem.

Nutritional abuse and eating disorders may result in undernourishment and dehydration. In particular, obese athletes are prone to hypertension (high blood pressure), diabetes, cardiovascular conditions and heat exhaustion, as well as psychological problems associated with being overweight.

Signals of common eating disorders:
- Anorexia
  - Rapid weight loss
  - Dieting, although thin
  - Poor self-image
  - Belief that body is fat (even when underweight)
  - Menstrual period stops
  - Unusual interest in food
  - Strange eating rituals
  - Eating in secret
  - Obsession with exercise
  - Depression
- Bulimia
  - Menstrual period stops
  - Unusual interest in food
  - Strange eating rituals
  - Eating in secret
  - Obsession with exercise
  - Depression
  - Binging (often without weight gain)
  - Purging (vomiting, diarrhea, excessive exercise)
  - Spending large amounts of time in the bathroom (to vomit)
  - Substance abuse

- Eating to bulk/compulsive overeating
  - Aggressive weight gain (generally fat over muscle)
  - Obsession with food
  - Consumption of large amounts of junk food
- Poor nutrition
  - Malnutrition
    - Unusually fatigued
    - Heat-related emergencies
    - Frequent injuries
  - Obesity

Eating disorders may become life threatening! The National Institutes of Health estimate that 10 percent of people with eating disorders die from starvation, cardiac arrest or suicide.

GUIDELINES TO PREVENT NUTRITIONAL ABUSE AND EATING DISORDERS

1. Understand basic factors about eating disorders, which are that:
   - Athletes with eating disorders often deny their problem and refuse help;
   - The earlier treatment begins, the greater the chance of full recovery; and
   - Treatment can be life saving.
2. Provide athletes with accurate, credible, up-to-date and relevant nutritional information.
3. Discuss nutritional abuse and eating disorders with parents.
4. Use caution when relating weight to performance. Seek advice from a trained nutritionist rather than suggesting dieting or weight increase.
5. Use caution when discussing weight or body fat with athletes. Seek advice from a sports psychologist or

nutritionist to avoid triggering eating disorders in athletes.

6. Seek expert advice if you notice rapid weight loss with any athlete.

7. Advise athletes who are dieting to seek medical nutritional advice: Stringent dieting can trigger eating disorders. Use of dietary supplements that have known adverse side-effects should be discouraged and avoided.

8. Discuss the hazards of bulking up and discourage the practice.

9. Seek expert advice for athletes who experience rapid weight increase.

10. Advise athletes who are attempting to increase weight to seek help from a physician, qualified trainer or dietician.

11. Discuss athletes' diets with them frequently to ensure that they are eating regular meals, that their diets are properly balanced and that they are not developing poor eating habits.

12. Try to schedule practices so that athletes can eat meals with their families.

13. Encourage athletes to drink fluids—especially water—continuously during training and competition, not only when thirsty.

14. Discourage athletes from eating candy for sugar highs.

15. Dispel the myth of the pre-game meal: Athletes should eat only easily digestible, high-carbohydrate, low-fat foods before competition—never high-protein, high-fat foods such as steaks.

16. Direct athletes to eat a balanced meal soon after training and competition.

17. Direct athletes' specific diet-related questions to nutrition professionals.

■ ALLERGIC REACTIONS

Severe allergic reactions are rare. But when one occurs, it is truly a life-threatening medical emergency. A severe allergic reaction, called anaphylaxis, is a form of shock. It can be caused by an insect bite or sting or by contact with drugs, medications, foods or chemicals.

IMPORTANCE FOR ATHLETES

An athlete with known allergies typically knows what to avoid and does so. The athlete may have a medical kit (epinephrine auto-injector) to treat an allergic reaction. Not all allergies are known by the athlete or can be prevented, however, so it is important to recognize the first signals of an allergic reaction and seek medical help immediately to prevent the problem from worsening.

Elite athletes should not take prescription or over-the-counter medications without first checking to see if it contains banned substances. The number for the U.S. Anti-Doping Agency Hotline is 1 (800) 233-0393.

Signals of Allergic Reaction
● Reaction occurs suddenly, within seconds or minutes after contact with the substance.
● Skin or body area in contact with the substance usually swells and turns red. Hives, itching and rash may occur.
● Breathing difficulty is common, including coughing and wheezing.
● Other signals are weakness, nausea, vomiting, dizziness, sneezing and bloodshot, swollen eyes.

See p. 72 on how to care for someone who is having an allergic reaction.

■ EXERCISE-INDUCED ASTHMA

Exercise-induced asthma is a medical condition that occurs when exercising causes swollen tissue to obstruct the airway, resulting in breathing difficulty, and sometimes, coughing, chest pain, chest tightness, or wheezing. Note that younger athletes may have exercise-induced asthma that has not been diagnosed and of which they are unaware. When not cared for properly, exercise-induced asthma may have a serious effect on an athlete.

See p. 90 for the care for someone having an asthma attack.

IMPORTANCE FOR ATHLETES

Fortunately, with most asthmatic athletes, the asthma may be controlled, allowing the athlete to train and compete with minimal discomfort or interference. Asthmatic athletes should not be discouraged from participating in sports.

■ PREVENTING SUBSTANCE ABUSE

From youth sports through professional competition, abuse of recreational drugs (including alcohol and tobacco products) and performance-enhancing substances (such as anabolic steroids) has become a significant problem. As a result, coaches need to recognize the signals of substance abuse and intervene promptly and effectively when substance abuse is suspected or known.

IMPORTANCE FOR ATHLETES

Substance abuse—whether with recreational drugs or performance-enhancing drugs—may have a detrimental impact on an athlete's performance, career, and lifestyle. Substance abuse may have serious long-term negative physical and mental side effects. Substance abuse also may result in an athlete being banned from athletic competition.

General signals of substance abuse include:

- Abnormal behavior;
- Mood swings;
- Argumentativeness;
- Resisting authority;
- Deceitfulness;
- Changes in appearance;
- Abrupt weight change;
- Stretch marks;
- Obsessive attention to body;
- Changes in performance;
- Altered concentration;
- Habitually early or late arrival at practice;
- High incidence of injuries;
- Heavy use of medication; and
- Needle marks.

Using anabolic steroids, growth hormones, stimulants and other performance-enhancing substances cheat honest athletes. These substances should not be used as they can be life threatening.

Use of anabolic steroids increases the risk of:

- Heart attack;
- Heart disease;
- Stroke;
- Kidney disease;
- Hepatitis; and
- Liver tumors.

Side effects of anabolic steroids in men:

- Breast development;
- Shrunken testicles;
- Impotence; and
- Excessive acne.

Side effects of anabolic steroids in women:

- Breast shrinkage;

- Clitoral enlargement;
- Infertility;
- Male-pattern baldness;
- Deepened voice; and
- Excessive acne.

Side effects of anabolic steroids in children:
- Possible impairment of growth; and
- Possible impairment of development.

Side effects of growth hormone:
- Bone deformity;
- Glucose intolerance;
- Hypertension; and
- Heart disease.

Side effects of stimulants:
- Headaches;
- Heart palpitations;
- Hypertension;
- Insomnia; and
- Nervousness.

GUIDELINES TO PREVENT SUBSTANCE ABUSE

1. Take the initiative in dealing with substance abuse and make it part of your athletic program.
   - Become—and stay—well informed about substance abuse:
     - Causes
     - Signals
     - Dangers
     - Intervention techniques
2. Become knowledgeable about performance-enhancing substances:
   - Steroids
   - Growth hormones
   - Blood doping

3. Know which drugs are banned for athletes:
   - Illegal substances
   - Ingredients of supplements
   - Over-the-counter medications (such as cold medicine and eye drops); and
   - To find out if a substance is banned, call the U.S. Anti-Doping Agency Hotline: 1-800-233-0393
4. Know which drugs are approved for training but not for competition.
5. Understand urine testing procedures.
6. Be aware of techniques for masking drug use.
7. Insist that all members of the coaching staff—assistant coaches, trainers, team doctors, and volunteers—learn about substance abuse, banned drugs and drug testing. Contact your sport's NGB for more information.
8. Keep continuously alert to the signals of substance abuse—both recreational drugs and performance-enhancing substances.
9. Provide effective, credible information to athletes on the use and abuse of recreational drugs (including alcohol and tobacco products):
   - Types of illegal or inappropriate recreational drugs
   - Side effects
   - Legal consequences
   - Penalties as an athlete
   - Signals
10. Provide effective, credible information to athletes and parents on the use of steroids, growth hormones, and blood doping:
    - Banned drugs
    - Signals of steroid use
    - Side effects
    - Penalties
    - Ethical consequences
    - Drug testing

11. Address personal prejudices about substance abuse that may prevent you from discussing it objectively.
12. If you choose to intervene when responding to substance abuse or the suspicion of substance abuse:
    - Carefully and privately document your suspicions;
    - If necessary, obtain assistance from a professional experienced with substance abuse;
    - If you talk to an athlete about possible substance abuse, do so privately and express concern about the athlete's health and well-being; and
    - If rehabilitation is needed, rely on professionals.

■ PSYCHOLOGICAL INJURIES

The stress to train rigorously and compete at a high level may result in psychological injuries—with both mental and physical signals—in athletes of all ages and in all sports. Stress may be caused by competition, coaches, parents or teammates or may be self-imposed by the athlete.

IMPORTANCE FOR ATHLETES

Psychological injuries caused by stress may have a significant and long-lasting impact on athletic activities and lifestyle. In the short term, psychological injuries may leave athletes emotionally unable to train and compete and may cause serious physical problems. In the long term, psychological injuries may affect athletes' self-esteem and quality of life.

Signals of stress:
- Muscle aches, pain and stiffness
- Headaches
- Nausea
- Rashes/hives
- Fatigue
- Inability to sleep

- Acute anxiety
- Hyperactivity
- Decrease in quality of school work (student)
- Poor job performance
- Eating disorders
- Depression

GUIDELINES TO PREVENT PSYCHOLOGICAL INJURIES

1. To prevent burnout, limit the amount of time during and outside the season that athletes can train without taking time away from the sport.
2. Use a coaching style that is appropriate for the age, experience and ability of athletes.
3. Ensure that the size, maturity and skill level of athletes are comparable.
4. Create an environment for training and competition that is fun and encourages sportsmanship.
5. Develop a training program that offers variety rather than repetition.
6. Be flexible.
7. Do not overemphasize the importance of winning.
8. Keep individual and team goals in perspective.
9. Use positive reinforcement techniques to motivate athletes, particularly younger athletes.
10. Communicate to parents, family members and agents the dangers of pushing young athletes too hard, as well as the stress that may result from overzealous behavior during competition.
11. To the extent possible and warranted, provide for non-sport diversions, such as social events.

■ PREVENTING DISEASE TRANSMISSION WHEN GIVING CARE

Some people are concerned about the risk of infection as a result of giving care to an injured person. It is important for you to know how diseases are transmitted and how to protect yourself when giving first aid.

Diseases that can pass from one person to another are called infectious diseases. Infectious diseases develop when germs invade the body and cause illness. The most common germs are bacteria and viruses.

Bacteria can live outside the body and do not depend on other organisms for life. The number of bacteria that infect humans is very small. When an infection is present, doctors may prescribe antibiotic medications that either kill the bacteria or weaken them enough for the body to get rid of them.

Viruses depend on other organisms to live. Once in the body, they are more difficult to remove. Few medications can fight viruses. The body's immune system is the best protection against infection.

In first aid situations, diseases can be transmitted from one person to another by touching, breathing and biting.

Germs in infected blood or other body fluids pass into your body through breaks or cuts in the skin or through the lining of your eyes, nose and mouth. Therefore the greatest risk of infection occurs when you touch blood or other body fluids directly.

Be careful when handling soiled objects. Sharp objects can cut your skin and pass germs. Avoid touching blood and blood-soiled objects with your bare hands. Some diseases, such as the common cold, are transmitted by air. Airborne infection can occur during sneezing, coughing and so on. Most of us are exposed to germs everyday in our jobs, on the bus or in a crowded restaurant. Fortunately, simply being exposed to these germs is usually not enough for diseases to be transmitted.

Some diseases are passed more easily than others. We all know how quickly the flu can pass from person to person at home or at work. Although these diseases can create discomfort, they are often temporary and are not serious to healthy adults.

Other diseases can be more serious, such as hepatitis B (HBV), hepatitis C (HCV) and human immunodeficiency virus (HIV), which causes acquired immunodeficiency (AIDS). Although very serious, they are not easily transmitted and are not passed by casual contact, such as shaking hands. In a first aid setting, the primary way to transmit HBV, HCV or HIV is through blood-to-blood contact.

By following some basic guidelines, you can help reduce disease transmission for both you and the injured athlete when providing care. These precautions, called "standard precautions," mean that you should consider all body fluids and substances as infectious:

- Avoid contact with blood and other body fluids or touching objects that may be soiled with blood or other body fluids.
- Use alcohol-based hand rubs to clean your hands where hand washing facilities are not available, but not in place of hand washing with soap and water.
- Wear protective clothing, such as disposable gloves, to cover any cuts, scrapes, and skin conditions you may have.
- Wash your hands with soap and water immediately after giving care.
  - *Using soap and warm water.*
  - *Lathering for at least 20 seconds.*
  - *Thoroughly scrubbing nails.*
  - *Using disposable paper towels for drying and turning off water.*
- Place barriers, such as protective eyewear, CPR breathing barriers, and disposable gloves (latex or non-latex such as vinyl or nitrile) between you and an athlete's blood or other body fluids.

- Remove jewelry such as rings and watches before providing care.
- Avoid eating, drinking, smoking, applying cosmetics or lip balm, handling contact lenses or touching your mouth, nose, or eyes when you may be exposed to infectious materials or giving first aid.

CLEANING UP A BLOOD OR BODY FLUID SPILL

If a spill occurs:
- Use disposable gloves and other personal protective equipment when cleaning blood or other body fluid spills;
- Clean up the spill immediately or as soon as possible after the spill occurs;

- Wipe up the spill with paper towels or other absorbent material;
- After the area has been wiped, flood the area with a disinfectant solution such as 1/4 cup liquid chlorine bleach to 1 gallon of fresh water, and allow it to stand for at least 10 minutes;
- Dispose of the contaminated material used to clean up the spill in a labeled biohazard container;
- Remember to always wash your hands whenever you may be exposed to blood or other body fluids.

Following these guidelines significantly decreases your risk of contracting or transmitting an infectious disease. Remember always to provide care in ways that protect you and the injured or ill person from disease transmission.

HEPATITIS B (HBV) TRANSMISSION

Hepatitis B is a liver infection caused by the hepatitis B virus (HBV). Hepatitis B may be severe or even fatal. The disease may be in the body for up to 6 months before signals appear. Symptoms may include flu-like signals such as fatigue, abdominal pain, loss of appetite, nausea, vomiting and joint pain. Later-stage symptoms include jaundice (a yellowing of the skin and eyes).

Although prevention of hepatitis B is important, there are medications available to treat chronic hepatitis B infections. These medications work for only some people. Hepatitis B vaccine prevents hepatitis B disease and its possibly serious consequences (such as liver cancer). This vaccine is given in a series of three doses to provide immunity. Hepatitis B vaccine is a safe and effective way to prevent hepatitis B disease. Scientific data show that hepatitis B vaccines are very safe for infants, children and adults. There is no confirmed evidence that indicates that hepatitis B vaccine can cause chronic illnesses.

HEPATITIS C (HCV) TRANSMISSION

Hepatitis C is a liver disease caused by the hepatitis C virus (HCV). It is the most common chronic blood borne infection in the United States. Its symptoms are similar to hepatitis B infection, including fatigue, abdominal pain, loss of appetite, nausea, vomiting and jaundice. There is no vaccine against hepatitis C, and no treatment after an exposure occurs that can prevent infection. It is the leading cause of liver transplants. For these reasons, hepatitis C is more serious than hepatitis B.

HUMAN IMMUNODEFICIENCY VIRUS (HIV) TRANSMISSION

AIDS (acquired immunodeficiency syndrome) is a condition caused by HIV (human immunodeficiency virus) and is the result of a weakened immune system. HIV attacks white blood cells and destroys the body's ability to fight infection. The infections that strike people whose immune systems are weakened by HIV are called opportunistic infections. Some opportunistic infections include severe pneumonia, tuberculosis, Kaposi's sarcoma and other unusual cancers.

People infected with HIV may not feel or look sick. A blood test, however, can detect the HIV antibody. When the infected person shows signs of having certain infections or cancers, he or she may be diagnosed as having AIDS. The infections can cause fever, fatigue, diarrhea, skin rashes, night sweats, loss of appetite, swollen lymph glands and significant weight loss. In the advanced stages, AIDS is a very serious condition. People with AIDS eventually develop life-threatening infections and can die from these infections.

Unfortunately, there is no vaccine against HIV. A vaccine could either prevent HIV infection or slow the progression of HIV in people who already have the virus. Most vaccines cause the body to make antibodies to destroy a particular germ if it invades the body. Such an approach has not yet been successful against HIV. Although progress in vaccine research makes some experts hopeful, a great deal more needs to be done. Adopting prevention behavior is still the best tool against HIV.

For additional information on these or other diseases, visit the Centers for Disease Control and Prevention (CDC) Web site at www.cdc.gov.

AFTER AN INJURY OCCURS

■ RETURN-TO-PLAY GUIDELINES

If an athlete has been injured or ill but seems to have recovered, you may need to decide whether the athlete can safely return to play.

IMPORTANCE FOR ATHLETES

The severity of an injury or illness is not easily determined. An injury or illness that is incorrectly identified and for which the athlete does not receive medical attention may become worse. If medical care is needed, returning to play may be inappropriate after an injury, and sometimes even "sitting it out" through the rest of the practice or competition may be inappropriate. Recovery time may be longer if proper care is delayed, and the athlete could experience increased or permanent damage.

GUIDELINES FOR RETURN TO PLAY

1. Discourage the athlete from returning to play if he or she feels unable to participate.

2. Check the Emergency Reference section of this handbook for actions to take with specific injuries and illnesses. In many cases, the athlete clearly needs medical attention.
3. Know and follow the guidelines for how and when to call 9-1-1 or the local emergency number (Part 2, p. 68).
4. The absence of pain does not signify the injury is not serious. Do not return an athlete to play simply because he or she says the pain is minimal.
5. With an injury causing pain, swelling or redness, do not ask the athlete to try to "walk it off." Movement may aggravate the injury.
6. Do not let the athlete move at all with any suspected injury to the head, neck or back. Do not let others touch the athlete or roll him or her over. Call EMS personnel immediately.
7. An athlete with any of the following signals needs immediate medical care:
   • Deformity of limb
   • Any extreme localized pain
   • Joint pain
   • Altered level of consciousness, including drowsiness, disorientation, seizure or unconsciousness
   • Repeated vomiting or diarrhea
   • Unequal pupil size
   • Severe bleeding
   • Breathing difficulty or breathing irregularly
   • Fluid leaking from nose or ears
   • Any eye injury affecting vision; and
   • Chest pain or pressure
8. When in doubt, play it safe and do not let the athlete return to play.
9. Only when none of the above conditions are present is it safe to allow an athlete to return to play. How-

ever, never try to advise a reluctant athlete to return. Any athlete who does return to play should be watched closely for any signal that the injury or illness is significant.

10. Following a serious injury or illness, return to play should be guided by a physician's recommendation. These include injuries or illnesses that have resulted in:
    - Unconsciousness;
    - Concussion;
    - Surgery; and
    - Missing more than 7 consecutive days of training.

    See p. 61 for a sample Emergency Care Permission form.

11. The athlete should be able to demonstrate a pain-free full range of motion in the injured areas before returning to play.

■ REPORTING AND DOCUMENTING INJURIES

All injuries and incidents must be documented and reported appropriately. The facility may already have a form for this purpose, or one can be developed from the following forms.

See p. 62 for a sample Instructions for Emergency Telephone Calls form.

See p. 64 for a sample Incident Report form.

■ TRANSPORTING AN INJURED ATHLETE

Whether you transport an injured athlete or wait for professional medical assistance depends on many factors, including the availability of professional medical assistance, the severity of the injury or illness and your judgment.

IMPORTANCE FOR ATHLETES

Simple athletic injuries, particularly to the upper extremities, generally are not problematic during transport. Serious injuries of the upper extremities; unstable fractures; head, neck and back injuries; possible internal injuries; and minor injuries of the lower extremities may require specialized skill when an injured athlete is transported to a medical facility.

GUIDELINES FOR TRANSPORTING OR MOVING INJURED ATHLETES

1. **DO NOT** move an athlete with a suspected head, neck or back injury. If you suspect a life-threatening injury or illness, always call 9-1-1 or the local emergency number rather than transport the athlete yourself.
2. **DO NOT** move an athlete if you have doubts about the seriousness of an injury, how to care for an injury or how to transport an injured athlete. Wait for professional medical help.
3. **DO NOT** transport an athlete yourself if you are unsure of the nature of the injury. In many cases, you should call EMS personnel rather than attempt to transport the athlete yourself. Check the care section of this handbook for actions to take with specific injuries.
4. **DO NOT** move an athlete until you immobilize musculoskeletal injuries.
5. **DO NOT** allow other athletes to provide assistance to an injured or ill athlete unless they are following your instructions.
6. **DO NOT** transport the injured athlete to a healthcare facility by anyone other than EMS personnel unless two coaches (follow local protocols) can accompany the injured athlete.

■ CRITICAL INCIDENT STRESS DEBRIEFING

An emergency involving a serious injury or death is a critical incident. The acute stress it causes for staff, especially the primary rescuer, may overcome a person's ability to cope. This is often called critical incident stress, and it may have a powerful impact. If not appropriately managed, this acute stress may lead to a serious condition called post-traumatic stress syndrome.

IMPORTANCE TO ATHLETES AND COACHES

A person suffering from critical incident stress may become anxious and depressed and be unable to sleep. He or she may have nightmares, nausea, restlessness, loss of appetite, and other problems. Some effects may appear right away and others only after days, weeks or even months have passed. People suffering from critical incident stress may not be able to perform well in their sport or job.

SIGNALS OF CRITICAL INCIDENT STRESS REACTIONS

- Confusion
- Lowered attention span
- Poor concentration
- Denial
- Guilt
- Depression
- Anger
- Change in interactions with others
- Increased or decreased eating
- Uncharacteristic, excessive humor or silence
- Unusual behavior

GUIDELINES TO COPE WITH CRITICAL INCIDENT STRESS

This type of stress requires professional help to prevent post-traumatic stress syndrome. Other things the person may do to help reduce stress include using relaxation techniques, eating a balanced diet, avoiding alcohol and drugs, getting enough rest, and participating in some type of physical exercise or activity.

INJURY PREVENTION BIBLIOGRAPHY AND RESOURCE LIST

Publications

Bergeron, J. David, and Holly Wilson Green, *Coaches Guide to Sport Injuries,* 1989, Human Kinetics Books, Champaign, Illinois.

"Chew or Snuff is Real Bad Stuff," 1993, National Cancer Institute, National Institutes of Health, Public Health Service, U.S. Department of Health and Human Services, Washington, D.C.

"Eating Disorders," 1993, National Institute of Mental Health, National Institutes of Health, Public Health Service, U.S. Department of Health and Human Services, Washington, D.C.

Feigley, David A., editor, *Coaches' Reference Manual,* The Rutgers S.A.F.E.T.Y. Clinic, 1994, Rutgers University, New Brunswick, New Jersey.

Flegel, Melinda J., *Sport First Aid,* 1992, Leisure Press, Champaign, Illinois.

"Guidelines for Youth Endurance Development," 1991, National Youth Sports Safety Foundation, Inc., Needham, Massachusetts.

Heyward, Vivian H., Advanced Fitness Assessment & Exercise Prescription.

Howley, Edward T. and B. Don. Franks, *Health Fitness Instructor's Handbook.*

Martens, Rainer, *Successful Coaching,* 1990, Leisure Press, Champaign, Illinois.

Martens, Rainer, Robert W. Christina, John S. Harvey, Jr., and Brian J. Sharkey, *Coaching Young Athletes,* Human Kinetics Books, Champaign, IL.

Martens, Rainer, and Vern Seefeldt, editors, *Guidelines for Children's Sports,* 1979, American Alliance for Health, Physical Education, Recreation and Dance, Washington D.C.

McArdle, William D., Frank I. Katch, and Victor L. Katch, *Exercise Physiology: Energy, Nutrition, and Human Performance.*

McCann, Sean, and Judy Nelson, "Eating Disorders," Olympic Coach Vol. 5. No. 1, 1995

Micheli, Lyle J., Sportswise: *An Essential Guide for Youth Athletes, Parents, and Coaches,* 1990, Houghton Mifflin, Boston.

Overuse Injuries: A Coach's Guide to Understanding Risk Factors, Recognizing Symptoms and Guidelines for Prevention, 1991, National Youth Sports Safety Foundation, Inc., Needham, Massachusetts.

"Preparticipation Physical Exams Fact Sheet," National Youth Sports Safety Foundation, Inc., Needham, Massachusetts.

Procopio, Deborah, "Doping: Considerations for Coaches," Olympic Coach, Vol. 4, No. 4, 1994.

Sports Injury Risk Management & the Keys to Safety, Coalition of Americans to Protect Sports.

"Statistics," National Youth Sports Safety Foundation, Inc., Needham, Massachusetts.

"Tips for Athletes," 1991, National Youth Sports Safety Foundation, Inc., Needham, Massachusetts.

Wadler, Gary I., "The Coach and Athlete Drug Abuse," Olympic Coach, Vol. 6, No. 1, 1996.

"Youth Sports Injuries Fact Sheet," 1994, National Youth Sports Safety Foundation, Inc., Needham, Massachusetts "Youth Sports Program Guidelines," 1994, National Youth Sports Safety Foundation, Inc., Needham, Massachusetts.

Organizations

American College of Sports
Medicine
P.O. Box 1440
Indianapolis, IN 46206-1440
(317) 637-9200

American Medical Society for
Sports Medicine
7611 Elmwood Avenue, Suite
203
Middleton, WI 53562
(608) 831-4485

American Orthopaedic Society
for Sports Medicine
6300 North River Road,
Suite 200
Rosemont, IL 60018
(847) 292-4900

American Physical Therapy
Association
Sports Physical Therapy Section
505 King Street, Suite 103
LaCrosse, WI 54601
(800) 285-7787

National Association for Sport
and Physical Education
1900 Association Drive
Reston, VA 22091
(703) 476-3410

National Athletic Trainers'
Association
2952 Stemmons Parkway
Dallas, TX 75247
(214) 637-6282

National Youth Sports Safety
Foundation, Inc.
10 Meredith Circle
Needham, MA 02192-1946
(617) 449-2499

National Governing Bodies

This book provides only general injury prevention information related to many different sports. Sport-specific injury prevention guidelines are just as crucial. Contact the appropriate National Governing Body for additional information related to preventing injury in that sport.

Olympic Division

ARCHERY
National Archery Association
One Olympic Plaza
Colorado Springs, CO 80909
(719) 578-4576

BADMINTON
U.S. Badminton Association
One Olympic Plaza
Colorado Springs, CO 80909
(719) 578-4808

BASEBALL
USA Baseball
Overlook Building
4825 Creekstone Dr. Suite 200
Durham, NC 27703
(919) 474-8721

BASKETBALL
USA Basketball
5465 Mark Dabling Blvd.
Colorado Springs, CO 80918-
   3842
(719) 590-4800

BIATHLON
U.S. Biathlon Association
29 Ethan Allen Ave.
Colchester, VT 05446
(802) 654-7833

BOBSLED
U.S. Bobsled and Skeleton
   Federation
P.O. Box 828 (421 Old Military
   Rd.)
Lake Placid, NY 12946
(518) 523-1842

BOXING
USA Boxing
One Olympic Plaza
Colorado Springs, CO 80909
(719) 578-4506

CANOE/KAYAK
U.S. Canoe and Kayak Team
P.O. Box 789
Lake Placid, NY 12946-0789
(518) 523-1855

CURLING
USA Curling
1100 Center Point Dr. (P.O.
   Box 866)
Stevens Point, WI 54481
(715) 344-1199

CYCLING
USA Cycling, Inc.
One Olympic Plaza
Colorado Springs, CO 80909
(719) 578-4581

DIVING
United States Diving, Inc.
Pan American Plaza, Suite 430
201 South Capitol Ave.
Indianapolis, IN 46225
(317) 237-5252

EQUESTRIAN
American Horse Shows
  Association
4047 Ironworks Pkwy
Lexington, KY 40511

FENCING
U.S. Fencing Association
One Olympic Plaza
Colorado Springs, CO 80909
(719) 578-4511

FIELD HOCKEY
U.S. Field Hockey Association
One Olympic Plaza
Colorado Springs, CO 80909
(719) 578-4567

FIGURE SKATING
U.S. Figure Skating Association
20 First Street
Colorado Springs, CO 80909
(719) 635-5200

GYMNASTICS (Artistic and Rhythmic)
USA Gymnastics
Pan American Plaza, Suite 300
201 South Capitol Ave.
Indianapolis, IN 46225
(317) 237-5050

ICE HOCKEY
USA Hockey
1775 Bob Johnson Drive
Colorado Springs, CO 80906
(719) 599-5500

JUDO
United States Judo, Inc.
One Olympic Plaza
Colorado Springs, CO 80909
(719) 866-4730

LUGE
U.S. Luge Association
P.O. Box 651 (35 Church St.)
Lake Placid, NY 12946
(518) 523-2071

MODERN PENTATHLON
U.S. Modern Pentathlon
  Association
8610 Broadway, Suite 260
San Antonio, TX 78217
(210) 822-1206

ROWING
US Rowing Association
Pan American Plaza, Suite 400
201 South Capitol Ave.
Indianapolis, IN 46225
(317) 237-5656

SAILING
United States Sailing Association (U.S. Sailing)
P.O. Box 1260 (15 Maritime Dr. 02871)
Newport, RI 02871-0924
(401) 683-0800

SHOOTING
USA Shooting
One Olympic Plaza
Colorado Springs, CO 80909
(719) 578-4670

SKIING
U.S. Skiing
P.O. Box 100 (1500 Kearns
   Blvd.)
Park City, UT 84060
(801) 649-9090

SOCCER
U.S. Soccer Federation
U.S. Soccer House
1801-1811 South Prairie Ave.
Chicago, IL 60616
(312) 808-1300

SOFTBALL
Amateur Softball Association
2801 N.E. 50th St.
Oklahoma City, OK 73111-
   7203
(405) 424-5266

SPEED SKATING
U.S. Speedskating
P.O. Box 450639
Westlake, OH 48145
(440) 899-0128

SWIMMING
U.S. Swimming, Inc.
One Olympic Plaza
Colorado Springs, CO 80909
(719) 578-4578

SYNCHRONIZED
   SWIMMING
U.S. Synchronized Swimming,
   Inc.
Pan American Plaza, Suite 901
201 South Capitol Ave.
Indianapolis, IN 46225
(317) 237-5700

TABLE TENNIS
USA Table Tennis
One Olympic Plaza
Colorado Springs, CO 80909
(719) 578-4583

TEAM HANDBALL
U.S. Team Handball Federation
One Olympic Plaza
Colorado Springs, CO 80909
(719) 578-4582

TENNIS
U.S. Tennis Association
70 West Red Oak Ln.
White Plains, NY 10604-3602
(914) 696-7000

TRACK AND FIELD
USA Track and Field
1 RCA Dome Suite 14-D
Indianapolis, IN 46206
(317) 261-0500

VOLLEYBALL
USA Volleyball
715 S. Circle Dr.
Colorado Springs, CO 80910-
   1740
(719) 228-6800

WATER POLO
United States Water Polo
1685 W. Unitah
Colorado Springs, CO 80904
(719) 634-0699

WEIGHTLIFTING
U.S. Weightlifting Federation
One Olympic Plaza
Colorado Springs, CO 80909-
   5764
(719) 578-4508

WRESTLING
USA Wrestling
6155 Lehman Dr.
Colorado Springs, CO 80918
(719) 598-8181

Pan American Division

BOWLING
USA Bowling
1631 Mesa Ave. Suite A
Colorado Springs, CO 80906
(719) 636-2695

RACQUETBALL
American Amateur Racquetball
   Association
1685 West Uintah
Colorado Springs, CO 80904
(719) 635-5396

ROLLER SKATING
U.S. Amateur Confederation of
   Roller Skating
P.O. Box 6579 (4730 South St.)
Lincoln, NE 68506
(402) 483-7551

TAEKWONDO
U.S. Taekwondo Union
One Olympic Plaza, Suite 405
Colorado Springs, CO 80909
(719) 578-4632

EMERGENCY CARE PERMISSION FORM (SAMPLE)

Athlete's name: _____

Sport: _____

As parent or guardian of the above named athlete, I hereby authorize the staff of _____ to provide care, including authority for medical transportation, in the event of injury or illness. I also authorize qualified medical personnel to provide emergency medical care in the event of an emergency.

Parent/Guardian: _____

Address: _____

City: _____

State: _____ Zip: _____

Daytime telephone: _____

Evening telephone: _____

Other authorized person to contact in emergency:

Relationship to athlete: _____

Daytime telephone: _____

Evening telephone: _____

Family doctor: _____

Doctor's telephone: _____

Athlete's allergies, chronic illnesses, medications taken, or other medical conditions: _____

Signed: _____

Date: _____

INSTRUCTIONS FOR
EMERGENCY TELEPHONE CALLS

Emergency telephone numbers

(dial _____ for outside line)

EMS: _____

Fire: _____

Police: _____

Poison Control Center: _____

Number of this telephone: _____

Other Important Telephone Numbers

Facility manager: _____

Facility maintenance: _____

Power company: _____

Gas company: _____

Weather bureau: _____

Name and address of medical facility with 24-hour
emergency cardiac care:

_____

_____

INFORMATION FOR EMERGENCY CALL

(Be prepared to give this information to the EMS dispatcher)

1. Location: _____
   - Street Address _____
   - City or Town _____
   - Directions (cross streets, roads, landmarks, etc.)
   _____
   _____
   - Exits and evacuation routes _____
2. Telephone number from which the call is being made _____
3. Caller's name _____
4. What happened? _____
5. How many people are injured? _____
6. Condition of injured person(s) _____
7. Help (care) being provided _____

Note: Do not hang up first. Let the EMS dispatcher hang up first.

Note: In cities with Enhanced 9-1-1 (911E) systems, it is still important to know the information above for communication to the dispatcher. In many buildings, the telephone system may connect through a switchboard that will show only the corporate address rather than the specific facility from which you are calling. With cellular telephones, 911E is not functional because there is no fixed location to identify on the dispatcher's screen, so sharing this information is the only way to provide it.

(Sample Form—post by telephone)

SAMPLE INCIDENT REPORT FORM

Date of report: _____   Date of incident: _____

Time of incident: _____

Facility Information

Facility: _____   Phone #: _____

Address: _____   City _____

State _____   Zip _____

Personal Data - Injured Party

Facility: _____   Phone #: _____

Name: _____   Age: ____   Gender: _____

Address: _____   City _____

State _____   Zip _____

Phone number(s): home: _____

                 work: _____

Family contact (name and phone #): _____

Date: _____   Time: _____

Incident Data

Location of incident: _____

Description of incident: _____

Was an injury sustained?   Yes ___ No ___

If yes, describe the type of injury sustained: _____

Witnesses _____

1. Name: _____   Phone #: _____

   Address: _____   City _____

   State _____   Zip _____

2. Name: _____   Phone #: _____

   Address: _____   City _____

   State _____   Zip _____

Care Provided

Did victim refuse medical attention by staff?   Yes ___ No ___

Was care provided by facility staff?   Yes ___ No ___

Name of the person who provided care: _____

Describe in detail care provided: _____

_____

Was EMS called? _____

If yes, by whom? _____ Time EMS called: _____

Time EMS arrived: _____

Was the victim transported to an emergency facility?_____

If yes, where? _____

If no, person returned to activity?   Yes___ No ___

If no, what was the referral action taken: _____

_____

Victim's signature (Parent's/Guardian's if victim is a minor):

_____

Facility Data

Number of staff on duty at time of incident: _____

Weather conditions at time of incident: _____

Playing surface conditions at time of incident: _____

Name(s) of staff involved in incident: _____

Report Prepared By:

Name (please print): _____

Position: _____

Signature: _____

Date: _____

EMERGENCY REFERENCE

PART TWO

In any emergency, always follow the same approach to caring for the injured or ill athlete. As soon as you recognize that an emergency exists, take action.

Follow these emergency action steps:
CHECK the scene for safety; check the injured or ill athlete.
CALL 9-1-1 or the local emergency number.
CARE for the athlete.

Calling for help is often the most important action you can take to help the athlete in need of care.

If the athlete is unconscious, call 9-1-1 or the local emergency number immediately.
- You may have to dial "9" or another digit to access an outside line.

Sometimes a conscious athlete will tell you not to call EMS personnel, and you may not be sure what to do. The following will assist you in determining the appropriate response.

Always **CALL** 9-1-1 or the local emergency number if the injured athlete:
- Is or becomes unconscious;
- Is confused;
- Has breathing difficulty;
- Is not breathing or shows no signs of circulation;
- Has persistent chest pain or pressure;
- Is bleeding severely;
- Has pressure or pain in the abdomen that does not go away;
- Is vomiting blood or passing blood in the urine or feces;
- Has a seizure, sudden severe headache, or sudden slurred speech;

- Has a seizure and is pregnant;
- Has a seizure and is diabetic;
- Appears to have been poisoned;
- Has injuries to the head, neck, or back;
- Has possible broken bones;
- Has severe burns; or
- Obvious deformity.

Also **CALL** 9-1-1 or the local emergency number for any of these situations:
- Fire or explosion;
- Downed electrical wires;
- Swiftly moving or rapidly rising water;
- Presence of poisonous gas;
- Vehicle collisions; or
- Athletes who cannot be moved easily.

If you are ALONE—

Call FIRST—(before providing care) if an athlete is unconscious and over age 8 **OR** unconscious, under age 8 with *known* heart problems.

Call FAST—provide 1 minute of care (before making the call) if the athlete is unconscious and under age 8, a drowning/submersion victim, suffers cardiac arrest due to trauma or is a drug overdose victim.
- If you are alone and caring for a child (ages 1 to 8) with no signs of circulation, *Call FAST* applies; giving one minute of CPR is recommended before taking other actions, such as calling EMS or attaching an AED.

◢ ABDOMINAL INJURY ◣

An abdominal injury may be open, where organs could be exposed, or closed, with the skin unbroken. Abdominal injuries can be serious because there may be significant internal bleeding or damage to organs. The goals are to check for and recognize the problem quickly, call for help immediately and provide care until EMS personnel arrive.

■ HOW TO PREVENT—

Always follow safe practices to help avoid injury *(see p. 2 for the General Principles to Prevent Injury)*.

■ WHAT TO LOOK FOR—

- Severe abdominal pain
- Protruding organs
- Bruising
- Rigid abdominal muscles
- Possible external bleeding
- Nausea
- Vomiting (vomit may include blood)
- Weakness
- Thirst
- Tenderness or a tight feeling in the abdomen

■ WHAT TO DO—

CHECK the scene for safety. CHECK the injured athlete, following standard precautions as appropriate.
CALL 9-1-1 or the local emergency number.
CARE:

If organs are exposed in an open wound—

1. **Do not** apply pressure to organs or push them back inside.
2. Keep the athlete lying down with the knees bent, if that position does not cause pain. Put a folded blanket or pillow under the knees to support them in this position.
3. Remove any clothing from around the wound.
4. Loosely apply moist, sterile dressings or a clean cloth over the wound.
5. Keep the dressing moist with warm water.

6. Place a cloth over the dressing to keep organs warm.
7. Give care to minimize shock (*p. 158*).

If organs are not exposed—

1. Keep the athlete lying down with knees bent, if that position does not cause pain. Put a folded blanket or pillow under the knees to support him or her in this position.
2. Minimize shock (*p. 158*).

See also Wounds (p. 179).

► ABDOMINAL PAIN OR DISCOMFORT ◄

Abdominal pain occurring after an injury may be a signal of serious internal injury, even if there is no open wound. Abdominal pain without an obvious cause also may be a signal of a serious injury or illness.

■ WHAT TO LOOK FOR—

- Athlete complains of pain in the abdomen.
- Bruising
- External bleeding
- Nausea and vomiting
- Pale or ashen, moist skin
- Weakness
- Thirst
- The athlete complains of a tender or tight feeling in the abdomen.
- Organs possibly protruding from the abdomen

■ WHAT TO DO—

CHECK the scene for safety. **CHECK** the injured athlete, following standard precautions as appropriate.
CALL 9-1-1 or the local emergency number if the abdominal pain occurs after an injury or if the athlete has severe

abdominal pain that does not go away within 10 to 15 minutes.

CARE:

1. Position the athlete on the back.
2. Allow the athlete to bend the legs slightly if that position is more comfortable.
3. Roll a coat or blanket under the knees.

If abdominal pain occurs without obvious cause—

4. **CHECK** for other signals.
5. If the athlete has other signals or if the pain is sudden or severe, check for the following problems and give additional care as appropriate:
   - Poisoning (p. 155)
   - Sudden Illness (p. 165)
   - Chest Pain or Pressure (p. 123)
   - Pelvic Injury (p. 149)

See also Abdominal Injury (p. 69) for open wounds to the abdomen.

◄ **ABDOMINAL THRUSTS** ◄

(See Choking—Conscious Adult or Child Athlete, p. 125)

◄ **ABRASION** ◄

(See Wounds—Abrasion, p. 180)

◄ **AIRWAY OBSTRUCTION** ◄

(See Choking—Conscious Adult or Child Athlete, p. 125)

◄ **ALLERGIC REACTIONS** ◄

Allergic reactions to certain food, medication, insect bites and stings, and contact with poisonous plants may cause severe problems, including swelling of the face, eyes and air passages, which may restrict breathing. A severe allergic reaction, called *anaphylaxis,* is a form of shock. Severe allergic reactions are rare. But when one occurs, it is truly a life-threatening medical emergency.

The goals are to check for and recognize the problem quickly, call for help immediately, and provide care until EMS personnel arrive.

■ HOW TO PREVENT—

- An athlete with known allergies typically knows what to avoid and does so.
- Not all allergies are known by the athlete or can be prevented, however, so it is important to recognize the first signals of an allergic reaction and seek medical help immediately to prevent the problem from worsening.
- Elite athletes should not take prescription or over-the-counter medications without first checking to see if it contains banned substances. The number for the U.S. Anti-Doping Agency Hotline is (800) 233-0393.

■ WHAT TO LOOK FOR—

- Reaction occurs suddenly, within seconds or minutes after contact with the substance.
- Breathing difficulty including coughing and wheezing
- Feeling of tightness in the chest and throat
- Swelling of the face, neck and tongue
- Bloodshot, swollen eyes
- Skin or body area in contact with the substance usually swells and turns red
- Rash, hives or itching
- Dizziness or confusion
- Weakness, nausea and vomiting

■ WHAT TO DO—

CHECK the scene for safety. **CHECK** the injured athlete for swelling and breathing problems, following standard precautions as appropriate. **CHECK** for a medical alert bracelet or tag.

CALL 9-1-1 or the local emergency number if the athlete has breathing difficulty or shows any of the signs of an allergic reaction.

CARE:

1. Help the athlete into the position most comfortable for breathing.
2. The athlete may have a medical kit (such as an epinephrine auto-injector) to treat an allergic reaction. Assist the athlete as needed with using this kit until help arrives. You may need to have special training in order to assist with this medication.
3. Be prepared to give additional care for breathing difficulty (p. 88) or other problems that may develop while waiting for EMS to arrive.

See also care steps for Poisoning (p. 156).

▶ **AMPUTATION** ◀

(See Wounds—Amputation/Avulsion, p. 181)

▶ **ANIMAL BITES** ◀

(See Bites and Stings-Animal Bite, p. 78)

▶ **ASTHMA** ◀

(See Breathing Emergencies—Asthma, p. 90)

ATHLETE

(See Checking An Unconscious Athlete—Adult or Child, p. 103)

AUTOMATED EXTERNAL DEFIBRILLATION (AED)

(See Checking An Unconscious Athlete—AED, p. 118)

BANDAGING

Bandages are used to hold a dressing in place on a wound and help protect a wound from infection, to maintain pressure on a wound to help control bleeding, to immobilize an injured body part, and to help reduce swelling in certain muscle or joint injuries.

Two commonly used bandages are roller bandages and elastic bandages.

ROLLER BANDAGE

A roller bandage used to control bleeding is called a pressure bandage.

1. Start by securing the bandage over the dressing.

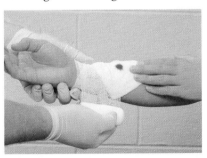

2. Use overlapping turns to cover the dressing completely.

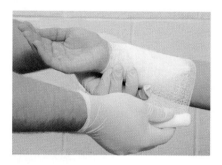

3. Tie or tape the bandage in place.

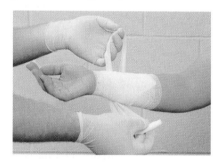

4. Check the fingers or toes for warmth, color, and feeling.

ELASTIC BANDAGE

Elastic bandages control swelling and give support for injuries such as sprains or strains.

1. Start at the point farthest from the heart.

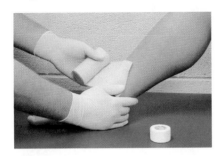

2. Anchor the bandage.

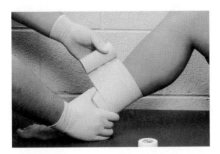

3. Wrap the bandage using overlapping turns.

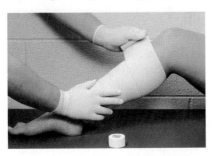

4. Tape the bandage in place.

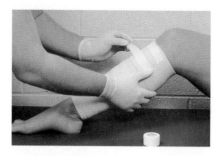

5. Check the finger or toes for warmth, color and feeling.

▶ BITES AND STINGS—ANIMAL BITE ◀

Animal bites can be serious. The goals of care are to control bleeding, get help for possible internal injury, and prevent infection. Remove the animal from the athlete, but do not try to capture it. Report what the animal looked like and the area where it was seen to authorities.

■ WHAT TO LOOK FOR—
- Bite mark
- Bleeding
- Pain

■ WHAT TO DO—
CHECK the scene for safety. **CHECK** the injured athlete, following standard precautions when appropriate.
CALL 9-1-1 or the local emergency number if bleeding is severe or other serious conditions exist.
CARE:

If bleeding is severe—
1. Control bleeding (*see Wounds—Bleeding, p. 182*).

2. Report the incident to the local animal-control officer or police.

If bleeding is minor—
1. Wash the wound with soap and warm water.
2. Control bleeding.
3. Apply antibiotic ointment, spray or cream.
4. Cover the wound.
5. Report the incident to the local animal-control officer or police.
6. Check with a doctor whether a tetanus booster may be necessary.

If you suspect that the animal has rabies, get medical attention, regardless of the severity of the injury.

See also Wounds—Bleeding (p. 182), Wounds—Puncture (p. 191), and Wounds (p. 179).

▶ BITES AND STINGS—BEE STING ◀

A bee sting may be only a painful annoyance or may become a life-threatening emergency for someone who has a severe allergic reaction. Since you cannot predict whether someone may be allergic, the primary goal of care is to watch for the signals of an allergic reaction and get help immediately.

■ WHAT TO LOOK FOR—
- Pain
- Swelling
- Possible signals of a severe allergic reaction—such as breathing difficulty, swelling or large rash (*see Allergic Reactions, p. 72 and Breathing Difficulty, p. 88*)
- Stinger stuck in skin

■ WHAT TO DO—

CHECK the scene for safety. **CHECK** the injured athlete; follow standard precautions.

CALL 9-1-1 or the local emergency number if the athlete shows signals of a severe allergic reaction.

CARE:

1. The athlete may have a medical kit (such as an epinephrine auto-injector) to treat an allergic reaction. Assist the athlete as needed with using this kit until help arrives. You may need to have special training in order to assist with this medication.
2. Remove the stinger by scraping it away with a credit card (or similar object).
3. Wash the wound with soap and water and bandage it.
4. Apply a cold pack, ice or other cold item. Place a cloth or towel between the skin and the source of cold.

▶ BITES AND STINGS—HUMAN BITE ◀

A bite from a human may be serious both because of the wound itself and because of the risk of infection. Microorganisms normally carried in the mouth may cause a serious infection if they enter the bloodstream. The goals of care are to call EMS personnel when appropriate, prevent infection, and care for the wound.

■ WHAT TO LOOK FOR—

- Bite mark
- Bleeding
- Pain

■ WHAT TO DO—

CHECK the scene for safety. **CHECK** the injured athlete, following standard precautions as appropriate.

CALL 9-1-1 or the local emergency number if the wound bleeds severely. If you suspect infection, advise the athlete to seek medical care, right away.

CARE:

If bleeding is minor—

1. Wash the wound with soap and warm water.
2. Control bleeding (*see Wounds—Bleeding, p. 182*).
3. Apply an antibiotic ointment, cream or spray.
4. Cover the wound.

If bleeding is severe—

1. Control bleeding (*see Wounds—Bleeding, p. 182*).

► **BITES AND STINGS—INSECT BITE** ◄

An insect bite may be only a painful annoyance or may become a life-threatening emergency for someone who has a severe allergic reaction. Since you cannot predict whether someone may be allergic, the primary goal of care is to watch for the signals of an allergic reaction and get help immediately.

■ WHAT TO LOOK FOR—

- Pain
- Swelling
- Marks on the skin or a stinger stuck in the skin
- Possible signals of an allergic reaction, especially breathing difficulty, swelling, hives or rash

■ WHAT TO DO—

CHECK the scene for safety. **CHECK** the injured athlete, following standard precautions as appropriate.

CALL 9-1-1, or the local emergency number if signals of an allergic reaction develop (*p. 72*).

CARE:

1. The athlete who knows he or she is allergic to bees may have a medical kit (such as an epinephrine auto-injector). Assist the athlete as needed with using this kit until help arrives. You may need to have special training in order to assist with this medication.
2. If there is a stinger in the skin, remove it with tweezers (if other than a bee sting) or by scraping it away with a credit card (or similar object).
3. Wash the wound with soap and water and bandage.
4. Apply a cold pack, ice or other cold item. Place a cloth or towel between the athlete's skin and the source of cold.

▶ **BITES AND STINGS—MARINE LIFE STING** ◀

Many types of marine life, including some jellyfish, stingrays, some types of coral, spiny urchins, and others, can sting swimmers and others in the water. If possible, ask local authorities what dangerous marine life may be present.

■ WHAT TO LOOK FOR—

- Possible marks on the skin
- Pain
- Swelling
- Possible signals of allergic reaction, especially breathing difficulty, swelling, hives or rash

■ WHAT TO DO—

CHECK the scene for safety. **CHECK** the injured athlete, following standard precautions as appropriate.

CALL 9-1-1 or the local emergency number if:

- Breathing difficulty or other signals of allergic reaction develop, such as swelling, or hives/rash (p. 73);

- The athlete does not know what caused the sting;
- The athlete has a history of allergic reaction to marine life stings; or
- The athlete is stung on the face or neck.

CARE:

If jellyfish sting—

1. Soak the area in vinegar.

If stingray sting—

1. Immobilize the area.
2. Soak the area in non-scalding hot water until pain goes away.
3. Clean and bandage the wound.

Note: *An athlete who knows he or she is allergic to marine life stings may carry a special kit (i.e., epinephrine auto-injector) or medicine. Assist the athlete as needed with using this kit until help arrives. You may need to have special training in order to assist with this medication.*

▶ BITES AND STINGS—SCORPION STING ◀

A scorpion sting may be only a painful annoyance or may become a life-threatening emergency in someone who has a severe allergic reaction. Since you can not predict whether someone may be allergic, the primary goal of care is to get help immediately.

■ WHAT TO LOOK FOR—

- Sting mark
- Pain or cramping
- Nausea and vomiting
- Breathing or swallowing difficulty
- Swelling
- Rash

- Profuse sweating or salivation
- Irregular heartbeat

■ WHAT TO DO—

CHECK the scene for safety. **CHECK** the injured athlete, following standard precautions when appropriate.
CALL 9-1-1 or the local emergency number; the athlete may need antivenin.
CARE:
1. Watch for the signals of allergic reaction, such as breathing difficulty, swelling, hives or rash (*p. 73*).
2. Wash the wound with soap and warm water.
3. Apply a cold pack or other cold object. Place a cloth or towel between the skin and the source of cold.

▶ BITES AND STINGS—SNAKE BITE ◀

The bite of four species of snakes in North America–the rattlesnake, copperhead, water moccasin, and coral snake–is poisonous, and in some cases the bite can be life-threatening. Do not try to capture the snake, but do note its appearance and provide this information to EMS personnel on arrival.

■ HOW TO PREVENT—

Be familiar with venomous snakes in your area and avoid their natural habitat wherever possible.

■ WHAT TO LOOK FOR—

- Bite mark
- Severe pain and burning
- Localized swelling and discoloration

■ WHAT TO DO—

CHECK the scene for safety. **CHECK** the injured athlete, following standard precautions when appropriate.

CALL 9-1-1 or the local emergency number unless you are certain the snake is a harmless species and the wound is minor.

CARE:

1. Keep the athlete calm and still.
2. Wash the wound with soap and warm water if possible.
3. Keep the bitten body part still and lower than the heart.
4. **Do not** apply ice to the wound.
5. **Do not** cut the wound to try to remove venom.
6. **Do not** apply a tourniquet.
7. **Do not** use an electric shock.
8. If possible, carry an athlete who must be moved, or have him or her walk slowly.

Note: If you cannot get professional care within 30 minutes and a snakebite kit is available, consider using the kit to suction the wound.

◄ BITES AND STINGS—SPIDER BITE ►

The bite of the black widow and brown recluse spiders in North America is poisonous, and in some cases the bite may be life threatening. Do not try to capture the spider, but do note its appearance and provide this information to EMS personnel on arrival.

■ WHAT TO LOOK FOR—

- Bite mark
- Blistering
- Swelling
- Profuse sweating or salivation
- Irregular heartbeat

- Pain or cramping
- Nausea and vomiting
- Breathing or swallowing difficulty

■ WHAT TO DO—

CHECK the scene for safety. **CHECK** the injured athlete, following standard precautions when appropriate.

CALL 9-1-1 or the local emergency number if you are unsure whether the bite was from a spider or other insect or if signals of an allergic reaction develop (*p. 73*).

CARE:

1. Wash the wound with soap and warm water.
2. Apply a cold pack or other cold object. Place a cloth or towel between the skin and the source of cold.

► BITES AND STINGS—TICK BITE ◄

A tick bite may transmit Rocky Mountain spotted fever or Lyme disease, either of which may be serious. The goals of care are to remove the tick from the skin safely and quickly and to watch for developing signals of disease. Not all ticks carry Lyme disease. Lyme disease is spread mainly by the deer tick, a pinhead-size tick found around wooded and grassy areas, and Rocky Mountain Spotted Fever is carried by the wood tick. Proper clothing and frequent checks for ticks can prevent tick bites. Signals of Lyme disease may develop slowly and might not occur at the same time as the rash. In addition, the rash does not always appear but Lyme disease may still be present.

■ WHAT TO LOOK FOR—

- Tick embedded in the flesh
- Sore, reddened area after the tick is removed
- Nausea
- Vomiting

- Severe headache
- Muscle pain
- Lack of appetite

Later signals of infection from tick bite—

- Fever, headache, weakness
- Abdominal Pain
- Diarrhea
- Flu-like joint, muscle pain
- Rash, which starts as a small red area at the site of the bite a few days or a few weeks after the bite:

On fair skin—

The center of the rash may be lighter in color, with the outer edges red and raised (bull's eye appearance).

On dark skin—

The area may look black and blue.

■ WHAT TO DO—

CHECK the scene for safety. **CHECK** the injured athlete, following standard precautions.

CALL 9-1-1 or the local emergency number only if the situation warrants it; seek medical attention if flu-like symptoms persist or rash occurs.

CARE:

1. With a gloved hand, grasp the tick with fine-tipped, pointed, non-etched, non-rasped tweezers as close to the skin as possible and *pull slowly.*

- **Do not** try to burn the tick off.
- **Do not** apply petroleum jelly or nail polish to the tick.
2. If you cannot remove the tick or if its mouth parts remain embedded, get medical care.
3. Wash the bite area with soap and warm water.
4. Apply antiseptic or antibiotic ointment.
5. If rash, flu-like signals or joint pain appears, seek medical attention.
6. Place the tick in a sealable container for analysis.
7. Wash your hands thoroughly.
See also Sudden Illness (p. 165).

► BLEEDING ◄

(See Wounds—Bleeding, p. 182)

► BONE OR JOINT INJURY ◄

(See Muscle, Bone and Joint [Musculoskeletal] Injuries, p. 147)

► BREATHING DIFFICULTY ◄

For breathing that has stopped, *(see Checking an Unconscious Athlete—Rescue Breathing—Adult or Child p. 105)* Breathing difficulty may be caused by many types of injury and illness. Since the problem may worsen and become life threatening, the goals are to check that a problem exists, call EMS personnel when necessary, and care for the specific problem. Common causes are listed below.

■ WHAT TO LOOK FOR—
- Unusually slow or rapid breathing
- Unusually shallow or deep breathing

- Gasping for air
- Wheezing
- Feeling short of breath
- Unusually moist or cool skin
- Flushed, pale, or ashen skin or bluish appearance
- Dizziness or lightheadedness
- Pain in the chest
- Tingling in the hands and feet

■ WHAT TO DO—

CHECK the scene for safety. **CHECK** the injured athlete, following standard precautions when appropriate.
CALL 9-1-1 or the local emergency number if the problem does not resolve itself immediately.
CARE:
1. **CHECK** for the possible cause of the problem; ask the athlete about allergies, medications, or conditions.
2. Help the athlete rest in a position comfortable for breathing.
3. Provide enough air: open windows and move bystanders back.
4. Continue to monitor the athlete's condition, and be prepared to give rescue breathing if needed (*see Rescue Breathing, p. 105*).

Any of the following may cause breathing difficulty. Look for additional signals of these problems and give the appropriate care:
- Allergic reaction (*p. 72*)
- Asthma (*p. 90*)
- Breathing Emergencies—Hyperventilation (*p. 93*)
- Chest injury (*p. 185*)
- Chest pain or pressure (*p. 123*)
- Choking (*p. 125*)
- Drowning (*p. 130*)
- Electrical burn (*p. 99*)

- Head injury (*p. 135*)
- Hyperventilation (*p. 93*)
- Poisoning (*p. 155*)
- Smoke Inhalation *(p. 159)*
- Substance abuse (*p. 163*)
- Sudden illness (*p. 165*)

▶ BREATHING EMERGENCIES—ASTHMA ◀

Asthma is a condition in which air passages become narrow, making breathing difficult. It can be a life-threatening emergency. An attack can be triggered by a reaction to food, medication, insect stings, emotional distress or physical activity. A young athlete may have exercise-induced asthma without being aware of it. Do not assume that an athlete with breathing difficulty is simply "out of shape." Any athlete, who seems to have unusual breathing difficulty, should be medically evaluated.

Coaches should be familiar with their athlete's medication and how to assist with its administration. A coach should assist an athlete with some or all of the steps of using asthma medication. The athlete should complete as many steps as possible themselves. The coach should assist only as needed, when:
- The athlete relates a history of asthma;
- The athlete states he or she is having asthma symptoms or an asthma attack;
- The athlete advises he or she needs assistance to use his or her quick-relief or rescue inhaler; or
- The athlete provides the quick-relief inhaler.

■ HOW TO PREVENT—
- Even asthma that is normally well controlled can cause airway obstruction after exercise.
- The likelihood of asthma or exercise-induced

asthma attacks depends on a number of factors, including:

- The athlete's health;
- How well the asthmatic condition is controlled;
- The intensity of exercise;
- The length of exercise; and
- Stress.
- Environmental conditions, such as cold, dry air and many airborne pollutants (e.g. tobacco smoke, pollen, etc.), increase airway obstruction.
- Medication may be needed prior to training or competing.
- A customized warm-up may be needed for an athlete who experiences exercise-induced asthma.
- Because conditioning improves breathing efficiency, better conditioned athletes in general will have a lower incidence of exercise-induced asthma.

■ WHAT TO LOOK FOR—

- Breathing difficulty
  - Shortness of breath
  - Chest tightness or pain
  - Wheezing
  - Rapid breathing rate
  - Inability to speak in full sentences
  - Gasping for air

- Dizziness or light-headedness
- Signals of shock (*see Shock—What to Look For, p. 158*)
- Coughing
- Rapid heart rate
- Sweating
- Tingling, numbness in fingers or toes
- Feelings of fear or confusion

■ WHAT TO DO—

CHECK the scene for safety. **CHECK** the injured athlete, following standard precautions as appropriate.

CALL 9-1-1, or the local emergency number if the breathing difficulty does not quickly resolve or for any asthma victim requiring assistance with an inhaler.

CARE:

1. Help the athlete rest in a position comfortable for breathing.
   - sitting upright or leaning forward
2. If the athlete has medication for asthma, assist him or her in taking it.
   - Ensure the prescription is in the athlete's name and is prescribed for "quick relief" or "acute" attacks. (**Note:** *some inhalers contain long-acting, preventive medication that should NOT be used in the event of an emergency.*)
   - Ensure that the expiration date of the medication has not been passed.
3. Stay with the athlete and watch for signals of breathing difficulty.
4. To minimize shock, keep the athlete from getting chilled or overheated.
5 Calm and reassure the athlete.

See also Breathing Difficulty (p. 88).

Hyperventilation is a breathing problem in which the athlete breathes faster than normal, resulting from fear or anxiety, certain illnesses, or injuries, such as head injuries or severe bleeding. Hyperventilation may be serious because it upsets the body's balance of oxygen and carbon dioxide. It may also be a signal of a more serious problem.

■ WHAT TO LOOK FOR—

- Rapid, shallow breathing
- Feeling of not getting enough air
- Fearful, apprehensive feelings
- Confusion or dizziness
- Tingling or numbness in the fingers and toes

■ WHAT TO DO—

CHECK the scene for safety. **CHECK** the athlete, follow standard precautions when appropriate.

CALL 9-1-1 or the local emergency number if there are changes in the level of consciousness or if breathing difficulty persists.

CARE:

1. Check for additional signals of serious injury or illness that may be causing the hyperventilation:
   - Asthma (*p. 90*)
   - Head, Neck or Back injury (*p. 135*)
   - Sudden Illness (*p. 165*)
2. Help the athlete rest in a position comfortable for breathing.
3. Provide enough air: open windows and move bystanders back.
4. Ask the athlete about allergies, medications or conditions.

Continue to monitor the athlete's condition and be prepared to give rescue breathing if needed (*see Checking an Unconscious Athlete—Rescue Breathing—Adult or Child, p. 105*).

▶ BREATHING—STOPPED ◀

(*See Checking an Unconscious Athlete—Rescue Breathing—Adult or Child, p. 105*)

▶ BROKEN BONE ◀

(*See Muscle, Bone and Joint [Musculoskeletal] Injuries, p. 147*)

▶ BRUISE ◀

(*See Wounds—Bruise, p. 185*)

▶ BURNS—HEAT/THERMAL ◀

See also Burns—Chemical (p. 98) and Burns—Electrical (p. 99). The care is different in some ways for these kinds of burns.

Burns are caused by heat, chemicals, electricity and radiation. The severity of a burn depends on the temperature of whatever caused the burn, the length of time the athlete was exposed, the location on the body, the burn's size, and the person's age and medical condition. Burns caused by heat are the most common. The goals of care are to stop the burning, prevent infection and get medical assistance when needed.

Superficial burns (1st degree)

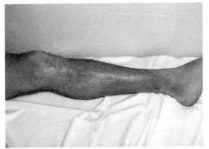

Alan Dimick, M.D., Professor of Surgery, Former Director of UAB Burn Center

- The skin is red and dry.
- The area may swell and is usually painful.

See Burns—Sunburn, p. 100

Partial Thickness (2nd degree)

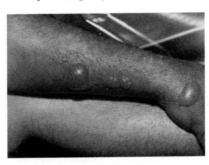

Alan Dimick, M.D., Professor of Surgery, Former Director of UAB Burn Center

- The skin is red and has blisters that may open and ooze clear fluid.
- The area may swell and is usually painful.
- The area may appear brown or black.
- The area may range from relatively painless to extremely painful.

Full Thickness (3rd degree)

Alan Dimick, M.D., Professor of Surgery,
Former Director of UAB Burn Center

- Destroys all layers of skin and any or all of the underlying structures—fat, muscles, bones and nerves.
- The area may appear brown or black with the tissues underneath sometimes appearing white.
- The area may be either extremely painful or relatively painless if the burn destroys the nerve endings.

■ WHAT TO DO—

CHECK the scene for safety. **CHECK** the injured athlete, following standard precautions when appropriate.

CALL 9-1-1 or the local emergency number for:
- Burns involving breathing difficulty;
- Burns covering more than one body part;
- Burns to the head, neck, hands, feet, or genitals;
- Burns (other than very minor) to a child or elderly person; or
- Burns resulting from chemicals, explosions or electricity.

CARE:
1. Stop the burning:
    - Remove the athlete from the heat source.

2. Cool the burn:

- Use large amounts of cool—not icy—water.
- Apply soaked towels, sheets or a wet cloth to the face or other areas that cannot be immersed.
- Keep the cloth cool by adding more water.
3. Cover the burn with dry, sterile dressings or a clean cloth.

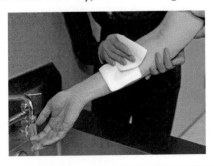

4. Loosely bandage the dressing in place to prevent infection and reduce pain or cover the burned area with a dry sheet.
5. Keep the athlete comfortable. To minimize shock, keep the athlete from getting chilled or overheated.
6. **DO NOT—**
   - Use ice or ice water except on small surface burns.
   - Put butter or other greasy substances on a burn.
   - Remove any pieces of cloth that stick to a burned area—medical professionals will clean the area.
   - Break blisters.
   - Put any kind of ointment on a severe burn.

For smoke inhalation, see p. 159.

BURNS—CHEMICAL

A chemical burn may occur anywhere there are chemicals and household substances, including cleansers, field maintenance supplies, or specialized chemicals, such as swimming pool chlorine. Because chemicals continue to burn as long as they are in contact with the skin, the goal of care is first to remove the chemical and then to care for the burn.

■ WHAT TO LOOK FOR—
- Presence of substance still on the skin
- Skin inflamed, red or any unusual color
- Pain, burning or stinging sensation

■ WHAT TO DO—
CHECK the scene for safety. **CHECK** the injured athlete, following standard precautions when appropriate.
CALL 9-1-1, or the local emergency number.
CARE:
1. Flush both the skin and eyes with large amounts of cool running water until EMS personnel arrive. Always flush away from the body.

2. Remove clothing and jewelry that may trap chemicals against the skin or on which chemicals may have spilled.
3. Keep flushing the affected area until EMS personnel arrive. Be careful not to come in contact with any chemicals yourself.

See also Burns—Heat/Thermal (p. 94).

BURNS—ELECTRICAL

An electrical burn may result from contact with electricity from a power line or cord, equipment or lightning. Do not approach an athlete who may still be in contact with electricity. Often the electrical shock causes problems more serious than the burn that occurs where the skin contacted the electricity, such as breathing or heart problems. Suspect a possible electrical injury if you hear a sudden loud pop or bang or see an unexpected flash of light.

■ WHAT TO LOOK FOR—

- Burn marks on the skin (entry and exit of current)
- Unconsciousness
- Dazed, confused behavior
- Breathing difficulty
- Weak, irregular or absent pulse

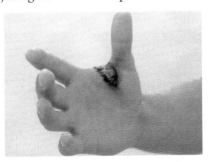

■ WHAT TO DO—

CHECK the scene for safety. **CHECK** the injured athlete, following standard precautions when appropriate.
CALL 9-1-1, or the local emergency number.
CARE:

- Never approach an injured athlete in contact with an electrical source until the power is turned off.
- If a power line is down, wait for the fire department or the power company.
- Check for breathing and other signs of circulation if the athlete is unconscious. Give rescue breathing (*see Checking an Unconscious Athlete—Rescue Breathing—Adult or Child, p. 105*) or CPR (*see p. 109*) if needed.
- Do not move the athlete unnecessarily; there may be internal injuries or a head, neck or back injury (*see p. 135*).
- Check for the possibility of two wounds: entrance and exit burns.
- Do not cool the burn area. *(This is different from heat burns.)*
- Cover the burn with a dry, sterile dressing.
- Take steps to minimize shock (*see p. 158*).

For a lightning strike—

- Look for life-threatening conditions, such as respiratory or cardiac arrest.
- Check for fractures, including back or neck fracture.
- Do not move the athlete.

See also Burns—Heat/Thermal (see p. 94).

▶ BURNS—SUNBURN ◀

Sunburn usually is a superficial burn and does not require emergency care. Prevention is important to avoid long-term effects of too much sun, such as skin cancer.

■ WHAT TO LOOK FOR—

- The skin is red and dry.
- The area may swell and is usually painful.
- The skin may have blisters that may open and ooze clear fluid.

■ WHAT TO DO—

CHECK the scene for safety. **CHECK** the injured athlete, following standard precautions when appropriate.
CALL 9-1-1, or the local emergency number if there are signals of a serious condition.
CARE:
1. Cool the burn.
2. Wash the area with soap and water and keep the area clean.
3. Prevent further damage by staying out of the sun or wearing a protective lotion or clothing.
4. Your doctor or pharmacist may recommend products for sunburn care.

If the skin blisters—

5. Protect unbroken blisters with loose bandages.
6. Keep broken blisters clean to prevent infection. Apply an antibiotic cream and watch for signals of infection.

▶ CHECKING AN ATHLETE FOR CONSCIOUSNESS ◀

Adult or Child

Unconsciousness, a state in which the athlete is completely unresponsive to touch and any sensory stimulus, is both a life-threatening emergency in itself and possibly a signal of a serious condition needing immediate care. Unconsciousness results from the brain not receiving enough oxygen, but this may be caused by a long list of injuries and illnesses. The goals of care are to get the athlete immediate medical help and care for whatever condition you find.

The athlete may not be unconscious when first found. An athlete whose consciousness level diminishes and then becomes unconsciousness usually signals a serious problem that requires immediate emergency medical care.

■ WHAT TO DO—

CHECK the scene for safety. **CHECK** the athlete, follow standard precautions as appropriate, for signals of possible causes of the unconsciousness:

- Chest Pain or Pressure (*see p. 123*)
- Choking—Conscious Adult or Child Athlete (*see p. 125*)
- Cold-Related Emergencies (*see p. 167*)
- Concussion (*see p. 135*)
- Electrical Burn (*see p. 99*)
- Fainting (*see p. 170*)
- Head, Neck or Back Injury (*see p. 135*)
- Heat-Related Emergencies (*see p. 171*)
- Internal Injury (*see p. 141*)
- Poisoning (*see p. 155*)
- Shock (*see p. 158*)
- Smoke Inhalation (*see p. 159*)
- Substance Abuse (*see p. 163*)
- Sudden Illness (*see p. 165*)
- Sudden Illness—Diabetic Emergency (*see p. 168*)
- Sudden Illness—Seizure (*see p. 172*)
- Sudden Illness—Stroke (*see p. 174*)

CALL 9-1-1 or the local emergency number even if the athlete regains consciousness because the athlete may still have a life-threatening condition.
CARE:
CHECK breathing. Position the athlete on the side to keep the airway open and allow fluids to drain from the mouth.

Adult or Child

■ WHAT TO LOOK FOR—

- The athlete may appear still, asleep or may not be moving.

■ WHAT TO DO—

CHECK the scene for safety. **CHECK** the injured athlete, following standard precautions.

CALL 9-1-1, or the local emergency number. If alone, provide one minute of care before calling 9-1-1 for a child.

CARE:

Tap and shout to see if the athlete responds.

If the athlete does not respond and is face-down—

Look, listen, and feel for breathing for about 5 seconds.

If the athlete is not breathing or you cannot tell—

- Position the athlete on his or her back while supporting the head and neck.
- Tilt the head back and lift the chin.

- Look, listen, and feel for breathing for about 5 seconds.

- Give 2 slow breaths.

- CHECK for signs of circulation for no more than 10 seconds.

- CHECK for severe bleeding.

If the athlete is unconscious, breathing normally, and no head, neck or back injury is suspected, place the athlete in a recovery position.

CHECKING AN UNCONSCIOUS ATHLETE

Rescue Breathing—Adult or Child

If an athlete's breathing has stopped, regardless of the reason, immediate action is needed to save the athlete's life. Brain cells begin to die within minutes. As soon as you determine breathing has stopped, give rescue breathing. Rescue breathing is somewhat different for children (ages 1 to 8) and adults (ages 9 and up).

■ WHAT TO LOOK FOR—

- Cannot see, feel or hear breaths
- The chest does not rise and fall
- The skin appears pale, bluish, or ashen

■ WHAT TO DO—

CHECK the scene for safety. CHECK the injured athlete, following standard precautions.

CALL 9-1-1, or the local emergency number immediately. If alone, provide one minute of care before calling 9-1-1 for a child.

CARE:

1. Tilt the athlete's head back and lift the chin. (Do not tilt a child's head back as far as an adult's.)

2. Look, listen and feel for breathing for about 5 seconds.
3. Be alert to special circumstances, such as loose dentures, possible head, neck or back injury, or neck stoma (*see p. 108 for modifying rescue breathing*) or for an object lodged in the throat (*see Choking—Unconscious Adult or Child, p. 114*).

If the athlete is not breathing—

4. Pinch the athlete's nose shut, open your mouth wide, and make a tight seal round the athlete's mouth.
5. Using a CPR breathing barrier give 2 slow breaths, until the chest clearly rises. If the breaths do not go in, reposition the airway by tilting the head further back and reattempt breaths. If air still does not go in, the airway is blocked (*p. 114*).
6. Check for signs of circulation (normal breathing, coughing or movement in response to rescue breaths or pulse) for no more than 10 seconds.

If the athlete is not breathing and shows signs of circulation—

7. Give rescue breaths.(Adult 1 breath about every 5 seconds for a Child 1 breath about every 3 seconds)

If the athlete is not breathing and does not show signs of circulation, start CPR (or use an AED if available) immediately (pp. 109-118).

8. Recheck for signs of circulation about every minute. Continue rescue breathing as long as a pulse or other sign of circulation is present but the athlete is not breathing. Check for signs of circulation every minute.
9. If the athlete vomits, carefully turn the athlete onto his or her side, wipe the mouth clean, and continue rescue breathing.

Modify rescue breathing in these circumstances—

Mouth and Jaw Injuries—Dentures

Loose dentures may interfere with rescue breathing. Dentures that do not remain in place and injuries to the mouth or jaw may make it difficult to make a tight seal around the mouth. If dentures do not remain in place, remove them. A mouth injury may cause the mouth to be tightly shut. Both situations require similar actions.

1. *With the athlete's head tilted back, close the mouth by pushing on the chin.*
2. *Seal your mouth around the athlete's nose.*
3. *Breathe into the athlete's nose (instead of the mouth) using the same procedure.*

If possible, open the athlete's mouth between breaths to let air out.

Head, Neck or Back Injury (see p. 135)

1. *If the athlete is not breathing, open the airway with the jaw thrust maneuver then give rescue breaths.*

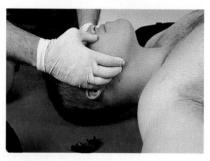

Mouth to Stoma Breathing

1. *Check for breathing at the stoma.*
   - *When giving rescue breaths, breathe into the stoma in the same way you would give breaths at the mouth.*
   - *You may need to seal the victim's nose and mouth to prevent air from escaping.*

CPR (Cardiopulmonary Resuscitation)

CPR is given to a person who is not breathing and does not show signs of circulation. CPR combines chest compressions and rescue breaths to circulate blood containing oxygen to the blood and other vital organs.

When to perform CPR:

- No breathing or other signs of circulation are present (cardiac arrest).

CPR is somewhat different for children (ages 1 to 8) and adults (ages 9 and up).

For CPR for adults, see below, for CPR for children (ages 1 to 8), see p. 111.

CPR—Adult (age 9 and older)

CPR is performed when the adult is unconscious, not breathing and shows no signs of circulation.

■ WHAT TO DO—

CHECK the scene for safety. **CHECK** the injured person for—

- Consciousness;
- An open airway;
- Breathing; and
- Other signs of circulation and severe bleeding.

CALL or have someone call 9-1-1 or the local emergency number.

If not breathing and no signs of circulation can be found, begin CPR:

1. Find your hand position in the center of the chest over the breastbone.

2. Position your shoulders over your hands with your elbows "locked". Compress the chest to a depth of about 2 inches, 15 times in about 10 seconds.

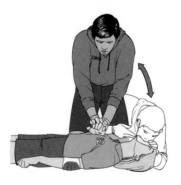

3. Give 2 slow breaths.
4. Repeat cycles of 15 compressions and 2 breaths for about 1 minute.

5. Recheck signs of circulation for no more than 10 seconds.

If there are no signs of circulation, continue sets of 15 compressions and 2 breaths until—

- The scene becomes unsafe;
- Signs of circulation return;
- An AED is ready to use;
- You are too exhausted to continue; or
- EMS personnel or another trained responder arrives and takes over.

Check for signs of circulation and breathing every few minutes thereafter.

CHECKING AN UNCONSCIOUS ATHLETE

CPR—Child (ages 1 to 8)

CPR is performed when the child is unconscious and not breathing and does not have signs of circulation (such as normal breathing, coughing or movement in response to rescue breaths or a pulse).

■ WHAT TO DO—

CHECK the scene for safety. **CHECK** the injured person for—
- Consciousness;
- An open airway;
- Breathing; and
- Other signs of circulation and severe bleeding.

CALL 9-1-1 or the local emergency number. If alone, provide one minute of care before calling 9-1-1 for a child.

CARE:

1. Check for breathing.

If the child is not breathing—

2. Tilt the head back, pinch the nose, using a CPR breathing barrier give 2 slow breaths. Each breath should make the chest gently rise.
3. Check for normal breathing, coughing or movement in response to rescue breaths or a pulse in the groove at the side of the neck.

If there are signs of circulation (such as coughing or movement in response to rescue breaths or a pulse) but no breathing—

4. Continue rescue breathing as needed.

If no breathing or other signs of circulation, begin CPR:

Find your hand position in the center of the chest over the breastbone. Place one hand on the child's chest and the other hand on the forehead to maintain an open airway.

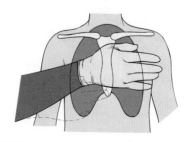

5. Position your shoulder over your hand. Compress the chest to a depth of about 1 1/2 inches deep, 5 times in about 3 seconds.

6. Give 1 slow breath.
7. Repeat cycles of 5 compressions and 1 breath for about 1 minute.

8. Recheck for signs of circulation for no more than 10 seconds.

If there are no signs of circulation, continue sets of 5 compressions and 1 breath until—

- The scene becomes unsafe;
- Signs of circulation return;
- An AED is ready to use;

- You are too exhausted to continue; or
- EMS personnel or another trained responder arrives and takes over.

Check for signs of circulation and breathing every few minutes thereafter.

CHECKING AN UNCONSCIOUS ATHLETE

Choking—Unconscious Adult or Child

The airway may become blocked by the tongue falling back in the throat or by food, objects, or fluids, such as blood, saliva, or mucus, becoming lodged in the airway. The care for unconscious choking is somewhat different for children (ages 1 to 8) and adults (ages 9 and up).

■ WHAT TO LOOK FOR—
- Athlete was observed choking when he or she was conscious.
- Breathing has stopped:
  - Cannot feel or hear breaths.
  - The chest does not rise and fall.
- The skin appears pale, bluish or ashen.
- Inability to make the chest clearly rise when attempting rescue breaths.

■ WHAT TO DO—
CHECK the scene for safety. **CHECK** the injured athlete, following standard precautions as appropriate.

CALL or have someone **CALL** 9-1-1 or the local emergency number. If alone, provide one minute of care before calling 9-1-1 for a child.

CARE:

1. Position the athlete on his or her back. Tilt the head back, lift the chin, and pinch the nose shut.
2. Using a breathing barrier, attempt to give 2 slow breaths.
3. If the athlete's chest does not clearly rise as you attempt to give breaths, reposition the athlete's airway by tilting the head further back, pinch the nose shut and give 2 rescue breaths again.

If air still does not go in—

4. Give chest compressions:
   - Locate the correct hand position for chest compressions. Only one hand is used for a child.

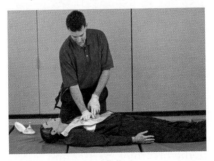

   - Position your shoulders over your hands with your elbows "locked."

- Give chest compressions:
- Compress the chest of an **adult** athlete to a depth of about 2 inches, 15 times in about 10 seconds.

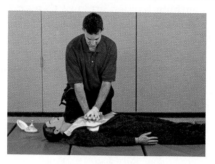

- Compress the chest of a **child** athlete to a depth of about 1 1/2 inches deep, 5 times in about 3 seconds.

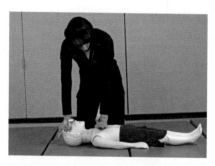

5. Look for a foreign object:
   - Remove the breathing barrier and open the athlete's mouth.
   - Look inside the athlete's mouth for a foreign object.

- If you see something, remove it with a finger.

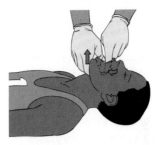

6. Replace the breathing barrier and attempt to give 2 rescue breaths (for a child, give 1 breath—if that breath goes in, give a second breath).

If breaths go in (the chest clearly rises)—

7. Check for signs of circulation (normal breathing, coughing or movement in response to rescue breaths or a pulse) for no more than 10 seconds.
   - If the athlete **has a pulse or shows other signs of circulation but is not breathing,** perform rescue breathing (*see Rescue Breathing—Adult or Child Athlete, p. 105*).
   - If the athlete **does not show any signs of circulation,** perform CPR (*see CPR, p. 109*).

If breaths do not go in (the chest does not clearly rise)—

8. Continue cycles of chest compressions (15 for an adult, 5 for a child), foreign object check/removal, and rescue breaths (2 for an adult, 1 for a child) until:
   - The scene becomes unsafe;
   - The object is removed and the chest clearly rises with rescue breaths;
   - The athlete starts breathing on his or her own;
   - EMS personnel or another trained responder arrives and takes over; or
   - You are too exhausted to continue.

Automated External Defibrillation (AED)

Ventricular fibrillation is a type of an abnormal heart rhythm. This abnormal heart rhythm occurs in adults and can affect young children. Defibrillation is an electric shock that interrupts the heart's chaotic electrical activity, and can restore the heart's ability to function as a pump.

An automated external defibrillator (AED) is a machine that analyzes the heart's rhythm and, if necessary, tells you to deliver a shock to a victim of sudden cardiac arrest.

An AED is used on a person who is not breathing and does not show signs of circulation. For using an AED on adults or children, see below.

Automated External Defibrillation (AED)— Using an AED on an Adult (age 9 or older)

■ WHAT TO DO—

CHECK the scene for safety. **CHECK** the injured athlete, follow standard precautions.
CALL 9-1-1or the local emergency number.
CARE:

To use an AED on *an adult (age 9 or older)*—

1. If the person shows *no signs of circulation*, turn on the AED and prepare it for use.

2. Wipe the athlete's chest dry.
3. Attach the AED pads to the athlete.

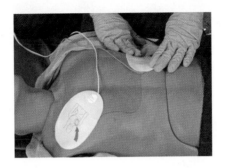

- Peel one pad at a time off the backing and, following the diagram, press the pad firmly to the adult's bare skin.
- Place one pad on the adult's upper right chest and other pad on the lower left side.
- Plug in connector, if necessary.
4. Make sure that *no one* is touching the adult.

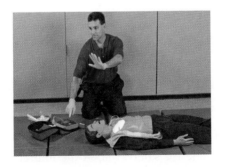

- Say, "EVERYONE, STAND CLEAR!"
5. Allow the AED to analyze the heart's rhythm.

6. Deliver a shock if prompted by pushing the "shock" button.

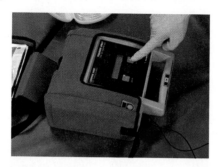

- Ensure that:
  - No one is touching the person.
  - No hazards are present, such as standing water
  - No is using a cell phone in the immediate area.
7. Allow the AED to reanalyze.
8. Re-check for signs of circulation, provide additional shocks or perform CPR (*see p. 109*) as necessary.

CHECKING AN UNCONSCIOUS ATHLETE

Automated External Defibrillation (AED)— Using an AED on a child (ages 1 to 8)

■ WHAT TO DO—

CHECK the scene for safety. **CHECK** the injured athlete, follow standard precautions.
CALL 9-1-1or the local emergency number. If alone, provide one minute of care before calling 9-1-1 for a child.

To use an AED on a <u>child</u> (ages 1 to 8, or less than 55 pounds)—

1. If there are *no signs of circulation*, turn on the AED and prepare it for use:

2. Wipe the person's chest dry.

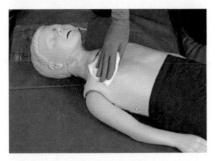

3. Attach the *pediatric AED pads* to the child, being certain they are *pediatric AED pads*.
   * Peel one pad at a time off the backing and, following the diagram, press the pad firmly to the child's bare skin;
   * Place one pad on the child's upper right chest and other pad on the child's lower left side as long as pads do not touch each other; if they do, use front/back (anterior/posterior) pad placement instead.

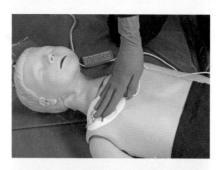

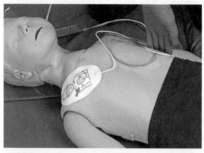

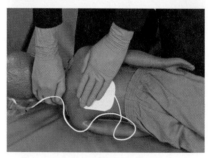

- Plug in connector, if necessary.
4. Make sure *no one* is touching the child
    - Say, "EVERYONE, STAND CLEAR!"
5. Allow the AED to analyze the heart's rhythm.

6. Deliver a shock if prompted by pushing the "shock" button.

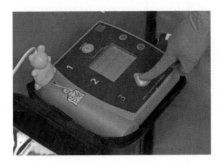

- Ensure that:
  - No one is touching the person.
  - No hazards are present, such as standing water; and
  - No one is using a cell phone in the immediate area.
7. Allow the AED to reanalyze.
8. Re-check for signs of circulation, provide additional shocks or perform CPR as necessary.

CHEEK INJURY

(See Wounds—Mouth and Jaw Injury, p. 144)

CHEST PAIN OR PRESSURE/POSSIBLE HEART ATTACK

Anyone can have a heart attack-even a conditioned athlete who seems in excellent health.

Most people who die of heart attacks die within 2 hours after the first signals appear. Many lives are lost because people deny they are having a heart attack and delay calling for help.

Recognizing the signals of a cardiac emergency such as a heart attack and quickly calling 9-1-1 or the local emergency number before the heart stops functioning are critical steps to saving lives. Also, knowing how to perform CPR and operate an AED are equally important since a heart attack can lead to a cardiac arrest.

Two common types of cardiac emergencies include:

- *Heart Attack:* this occurs when the heart does not function properly, denying the heart muscle of much needed oxygen and causing chest pain.
- *Cardiac Arrest:* This occurs when the heart does not function at all (*see Checking an Unconscious Athlete—CPR, p. 109 or AED, p. 120*)

■ WHAT TO LOOK FOR—

- Persistent chest pain or pressure (a primary signal of a heart attack) that lasts longer than 3-5 minutes, or goes away and comes back;
- Chest pain spreading to the shoulders, neck jaw or arms;
- Shortness of breath or trouble breathing;
- Nausea or vomiting;
- Dizziness, lightheadedness or fainting;
- Pale, ashen (grayish) or bluish skin;
- Sweating;
- Denial; and
- Women are somewhat more likely to experience some of the other warning signs, particularly shortness of breath, nausea, vomiting and back or jaw pain.

■ WHAT TO DO—

CHECK the scene for safety. **CHECK** the injured athlete, following standard precautions when appropriate.

CALL 9-1-1 or the local emergency number immediately.

CARE:

1. Have the person stop activity and rest in a comfortable position. A sitting position may make breathing easier.
2. Loosen restrictive clothing.
3. Assist with prescribed medication.
4. Monitor breathing and other signs of circulation closely.
5. Be prepared to give CPR and/or use an AED if the athlete stops breathing and has no other signs of circulation (*pp. 109/120*).

CHEST INJURY

(See Wounds—Chest Injuries, p. 185)

CHOKING

Conscious Adult or Child Athlete

Common causes of choking include: trying to swallow large pieces of poorly-chewed food; drinking alcohol before and during meals dulls the nerves that aid in swallowing; eating while talking excitedly or laughing; eating too fast; and walking, playing, or running with food or objects in the mouth. An injured athlete may also choke on dislodged teeth, vomit, or blood.

■ WHAT TO LOOK FOR—

- Cannot cough, speak or breathe
- High-pitched wheezing noise

■ WHAT TO DO—

CHECK the scene for safety. **CHECK** the injured athlete, following standard precautions when appropriate.

CALL 9-1-1 or the local emergency number if the athlete continues to cough without clearing the obstruction, cannot speak or cough, or becomes unconscious.
CARE:

For a choking athlete who can speak or cough—

Encourage the athlete to keep coughing to clear the obstruction.

Be prepared to give abdominal thrusts if person cannot cough forcefully, speak or breathe.

For a choking athlete who CANNOT cough forcefully, speak or breathe—

■ WHAT TO DO—

CHECK the scene for safety. **CHECK** the injured athlete, following standard precautions as appropriate.
CALL—have someone call 9-1-1 or the local emergency number.
CARE:
1. Get permission to give care.
2. Perform abdominal thrusts (Heimlich maneuver):
   • Place thumb side of fist against middle of abdomen just above the navel. Grasp fist with other hand.

- Give quick, upward thrusts.

3. Repeat abdominal thrusts until the—
   - Object is coughed up;
   - Athlete breathes on his or her own; or
   - Athlete becomes unconscious.

If the athlete becomes unconscious—

Carefully help the athlete to the floor. Then check for an object in the mouth. If the object is visible, remove it with a finger. Whether or not an object is removed, continue with the modified CPR technique for an unconscious choking athlete (see p. 114).

If you are alone and choking—

You can give yourself abdominal thrusts by leaning over a firm object, such as the back of a chair, and pressing your abdomen into it.

If a person is pregnant or too large for you to give abdominal thrusts—

Give chest thrusts. To give chest thrusts, grab your fist with your other hand, place the thumb side of your fist on the center of the breastbone, and give quick thrusts into the chest.

COLD-RELATED EMERGENCIES

(See Sudden Illness—Cold-Related Emergencies, p. 167)

COMPOUND (OR "OPEN") FRACTURE

(See Muscle, Bone and Joint [Musculoskeletal] Injury, p. 147)

CONCUSSION

(See Head, Neck or Back Injury, p. 135)

CONFUSION

Confusion without an obvious cause may be a signal of a serious condition. Check for other signals. If the athlete's confusion is without explanation, is especially severe or if the athlete has other signals, the athlete may have a serious condition. Send someone to call EMS personnel.

While waiting for EMS personnel, look for signals of any of the following conditions that may be possible causes of the confusion, and care for any problem found:

- Allergic Reactions (*p. 72*)
- Chest Pain or Pressure (*p. 123*)
- Cold-Related Emergencies (*p. 167*)
- Electrical Burn (*p. 99*)
- Head, Neck or Back Injury (*p. 135*)
- Heat-related Emergencies (*p. 171*)
- Hyperventilation (*p. 93*)
- Poisoning (*p. 155*)
- Shock (*p. 158*)
- Substance Abuse (*p. 163*)
- Sudden Illness-Diabetic Emergency (*p. 168*)
- Sudden Illness-Stroke (*p. 174*)

Unless you suspect a specific condition requiring additional care, give the care for Sudden Illness (*p. 165*).

CPR—ADULT OR CHILD

(See Checking an Unconscious Athlete—CPR, p. 109)

CRAMPS

(See Muscle, Injury—Cramps or Sudden Illness-Heat-Related Injuries, pp. 151/172)

CUTS

(See Wounds—Bleeding, p. 182)

DEHYDRATION

(See Preventing Dehydration, p. 31 and Sudden Illness-Heat-Related Emergencies, p. 171)

DIABETIC EMERGENCY

(See Sudden Illness—Diabetic Emergency, p. 168)

DIARRHEA

(See Sudden Illness—Diarrhea, p. 169)

DISLOCATION

(See Muscle, Bone and Joint [Musculoskeletal] Injuries, p. 147)

In a dislocation, the bone has been displaced from its normal position in a joint. This may be a serious injury. Because only an expert can tell the difference between a fracture and a dislocation, the care given while waiting for EMS personnel is the same.

DIZZINESS

Feeling dizzy may be a signal of a number of serious conditions, such as the conditions listed below. Look for additional signals that suggest any of these conditions and take the appropriate steps described in these sections:

- Allergic Reactions (*p. 77*)
- Breathing Emergencies—Hyperventilation (*p. 93*)
- Burns—Electrical (*p. 99*)
- Chest Pain or Pressure (*p. 123*)
- Cold-related Emergencies (*p. 167*)
- Electrical Burn (*p. 99*)
- Head, Neck, or Back injury (*p. 135*)
- Heat-related Emergencies (*p. 171*)
- Poisoning (*p. 155*)
- Shock (*p. 158*)
- Substance Abuse (*p. 163*)
- Sudden Illness (*p. 165*)
- Sudden Illness—Diabetic Emergency (*p. 168*)
- Sudden Illness—Stroke (*p. 174*)

See also the care for Fainting (p. 170).

DROWNING (NEAR-DROWNING)

Drowning may happen to anyone in, on, or around the water, regardless of how good a swimmer the athlete is or the nature of the activity. Being able to recognize an athlete who is having trouble in the water may help save the athlete's life. Since the athlete may not be able to call for help, it is important to know the signals of an emergency.

■ WHAT TO LOOK FOR—

- Struggling movements; little or no forward progress.
- The athlete may or may not be able to call or signal for help.
- The athlete struggles to breathe.

■ WHAT TO DO—

CHECK the scene for safety.
CALL 9-1-1 or the local emergency number.
CARE:

1. Attempt to rescue by reaching or throwing a floating object to the athlete (*see Water Rescue Methods on next page*). Do not attempt a swimming rescue unless trained to do so.

Once the athlete is out of the water—

2. CHECK the athlete, follow standard precautions as appropriate.
3. If the athlete is unconscious, tilt the head back and check for breathing. If not breathing, give 2 slow rescue breaths (*see Rescue Breathing, p. 105*).
4. If breaths do not go in, reposition the airway by tilting the head further back and try breaths again.
   - If breaths do not go in, give care for choking (*p. 114*).
5. If breaths go in, check for signs of circulation (normal breathing, coughing or movement in response to rescue breaths or a pulse). If none present, give CPR (*p. 109*).

Water Rescue Methods

The safest methods are reaching, throwing and wading assists. In most cases, at least one of these methods will be successful.

Reaching Assist

Throwing Assist

Wading Assist

DRUG OVERDOSE

(See Substance Abuse, p. 163)

EAR INJURY

(See Wounds— Ear Injury, p. 187)

ELECTRICAL BURN

(See Burns—Electrical, p. 99)

ELECTRICAL SHOCK

(See Burns—Electrical, p. 100)

EMBEDDED OBJECT

(See Wounds—Embeded Object, p. 187)

EYE INJURY

(See Wounds—Eye Injury, p. 189)

FAINTING

(See Sudden Illness—Fainting, p. 170)

FRACTURE

(See Muscle, Bone and Joint [Musculoskeletal] Injuries, p. 147)

Frostbite is a cold-related emergency. It may quickly become life or limb threatening. Frostbite is the freezing of a specific body area. (*see Sudden Illness—Cold-Related Emergencies, p. 167*)

■ WHAT TO LOOK FOR—

- Lack of feeling in the affected area
- Skin appears waxy, is cold to the touch, or is discolored (flushed, white or gray, yellow or blue)

■ WHAT TO DO—

CHECK the scene for safety. **CHECK** the injured athlete, following standard precautions when appropriate.
CALL 9-1-1 or the local emergency number.
CARE:
1. Handle the area gently; never rub the affected area.
2. Warm gently by soaking the affected area in warm water (100–105 degrees F) until it appears red and feels warm.

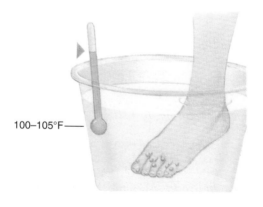

100–105°F

3. Loosely bandage the area with dry, sterile dressings.
4. If the athlete's fingers or toes are frostbitten, place dry, sterile gauze between them to keep them separated.
5. Avoid breaking any blisters.

HEADACHE

Headache without an obvious cause may be a signal of a serious condition. Check for other signals. If the athlete's headache is sudden, without explanation or severe, or if the athlete has other signals, consider the problems listed here and care for the appropriate problem:

- Head, Neck or Back Injury (below)
- Heat exhaustion or heat stroke (p. 172)
- Lyme disease (p. 86)
- Poisoning (p. 155)
- Sudden illness (p. 165)
- Sudden illness–Stroke (p. 174)

HEAD, NECK OR BACK INJURY

Although injuries to the head, neck or back account for only a small percentage of all injuries, they cause more than half of all injury-related deaths. Signals of a head, neck or back injury may be sometimes slow to develop and are not always noticeable at first. Always consider a possible head, neck or back injury seriously. A primary goal of care is to prevent further injury caused by movement until EMS personnel arrive.

Always suspect a head, neck or back injury in these situations:

- Any athlete thrown (such as from an animal or a moving vehicle) with sufficient force that creates a

significantly hard contact with floor boards, ground or objects, especially with the crown or top of the head
- A fall from a height greater than the athlete's height
- Any diving accident
- An athlete found unconscious for unknown reasons
- Any injury involving severe blunt force to the head, neck or back such as in football or boxing
- Any injury that penetrates the head or trunk, such as track shoe spike wounds or a gunshot wound
- A motor vehicle crash involving a driver or passengers not wearing safety belts
- Any injury in which an athlete's helmet is broken, including a hockey, football or cycling helmet
- Any incident involving a lightning strike

■ HOW TO PREVENT

Should an injury involve the head, neck or back, recognize the potential for serious injury and respond to prevent further injury to the spinal cord.

■ WHAT TO LOOK FOR—

- Changes in consciousness or loss of balance
- Sudden loss of memory
- Seizures in an athlete who does not have a seizure disorder
- Severe pain or pressure in the head, neck or back
- Tingling or loss of sensation in the hands, fingers, feet or toes
- Partial or complete loss of movement of any body part
- Unusual bumps or depressions on the head or over the spine

- Blood or other body fluids draining from the ears or nose
- Heavy external bleeding from the head, neck or back
- Impaired breathing or vision as a result of injury
- Nausea, vomiting or persistent headache
- Bruising of the head, especially around the eyes and behind the ears

■ WHAT TO DO—

CHECK the scene for safety. **CHECK** the injured athlete for consciousness and breathing, following standard precautions as appropriate.
CALL 9-1-1 or the local emergency number.
CARE:

If the athlete is unconscious—

1. Do not move the athlete unless absolutely necessary. If the athlete must be moved, do it carefully without twisting or bending the body. If alone, use the athlete's clothes to drag the athlete to safety while supporting the head and neck in line with the spine. Support the athlete's head in line with the body until EMS arrives.
   - If the athlete is not breathing, open the airway with the jaw thrust maneuver (p. 108) and give 2 slow rescue breaths.
2. Check for normal breathing and other signs of circulation (i.e., coughing and movement in response to rescue breaths or a pulse) for no more than 10 seconds. Give rescue breathing (see *Checking an Unconscious Athlete—Rescue Breathing, p. 105, CPR (p. 109) or AED (p. 118)*, as necessary.

If the athlete is conscious—

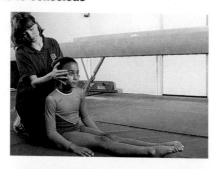

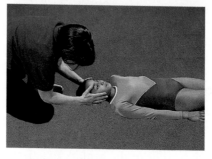

1. Support the athlete's head and neck in line with the body until EMS arrives.
2. Minimize movement of the head, neck and back.
3. Control any bleeding (see Wounds—Bleeding, p. 182).
4. To minimize shock, keep the athlete from getting chilled or overheated.

Note: Coaches should be aware that any injury to the head, neck, or back has the potential to be serious or life threatening. If there is any question regarding the extent of the injury, call 9-1-1 or the local emergency number.

HEART ATTACK

(See Chest Pain or Pressure/Possible Heart Attack, p. 123)

HEAT CRAMPS

(See Muscle Injury—Cramps, p. 151)

HEAT EXHAUSTION

(See Sudden Illness—Heat-Related Emergencies, p. 171)

HEAT-RELATED EMERGENCIES

(See Sudden Illness—Heat-Related Emergencies, p. 171)

HEAT STROKE

(See Sudden Illness—Heat-Related Emergencies, p. 171)

HEIMLICH MANEUVER

(See Choking—Conscious Adult or Child Athlete, p. 125)

HIVES

(See Allergic Reactions, p. 72)

HUMAN BITE

(See Bites and Stings—Human Bites, p. 80)

HYPERVENTILATION

(See Breathing Emergencies—Hyperventilation, p. 93)

(See Sudden Illness—Cold-Related Emergencies, p. 167)

INFECTION—PREVENTION

Harmful microorganisms may enter the body through scrapes, cuts or punctures and cause infection. Infection may develop within hours or days of an injury.

■ HOW TO PREVENT—

Follow standard precautions (see "Preventing Disease Transmission When Giving Care" p. 43)—

1. Wash hands before and after caring for the wound, even if you wear gloves.
2. Wash minor wounds with soap and water.
3. Do not wash wounds that require medical attention unless instructed to do so by a medical professional.
4. Cover the wound with a clean dressing and bandage; change daily.
5. If infection persists or worsens, have the athlete seek medical help.

■ WHAT TO LOOK FOR—

- The wound area becomes swollen and red.

- The area may feel warm or throb with pain.
- The area may discharge pus.
- Red streaks may develop around the wound.
- The athlete may develop a fever and feel ill.
- Seek medical attention for any developing infection.

▶ INJURY (See specific body areas injured) ◀

Abdominal Injury (*p. 69*)
Bone or Joint Injury (*p. 147*)
Muscle Injury (*pp. 150-153*)
Bruise (*see Wounds—Bruise, p. 185*)
Cheek Injury (*see Mouth and Jaw Injury, p. 145*)
Chest Injury (*see Wounds—Chest Injury, p. 186*)
Cuts (*see Wounds, p. 179*)
Ear Injury (*see Wounds—Ear Injury, p. 187*)
Eye Injury (*see Wounds—Eye Injury, p. 189*)
Head, Neck or Back Injury (*p. 135*)
Mouth Injury (*see Mouth and Jaw Injury, p. 144*)
Pelvic Injury (*see Muscle, Bone and Joint Injuries—Pelvic Injury, p. 149*)
Scalp Injury (*see Wounds—Scalp Injury, p. 193*)

▶ INSECT BITE ◀

(*See Bites and Stings—Insect bite, p. 81*)

▶ INTERNAL INJURY ◀

Internal injuries include internal bleeding and injury to organs. Such injuries may result from blunt blows to the body. Internal injury may be more difficult to recognize because the signals may develop more gradually, yet these injuries may be life threatening. The goals of first aid are to recognize when there may be an internal injury and provide care while waiting for EMS personnel to arrive.

■ WHAT TO LOOK FOR—

- Bruising in area
- Tender, swollen, or hard area (such as abdomen)
- Anxiety or restlessness
- Rapid, weak pulse
- Rapid breathing
- Skin that feels cool or moist or looks pale, bluish or ashen
- Nausea
- Vomiting blood or coughing up blood
- Excessive thirst
- Change in the level of consciousness (confused, faint, drowsy or unconscious)

■ WHAT TO DO—

CHECK the scene for safety. **CHECK** the injured athlete, following standard precautions when appropriate.
CALL 9-1-1 or the local emergency number if the situation warrants it.
CARE:
1. Help the athlete rest in the most comfortable position.
2. To minimize shock, keep the athlete from getting chilled or overheated (*p. 158*).
3. Reassure the athlete.
See also Abdominal Injury (p. 69), Wounds—Chest Injury (p. 186), Muscle, Bone and Joint Injuries—Pelvic, (p. 149), and Head, Neck, or Back Injury (p. 135)

▶ ITCHING ◀

(See Allergic Reactions, p. 72)

JELLYFISH STING

(See Bites and Stings—Marine Life Sting, p. 82)

JOINT INJURY

(See Muscle, Bone and Joint [Musculoskeletal] Injuries, p. 147)

LIGHTNING STRIKE

(See Burns—Electrical, p. 99)

LOSS OF SENSATION

A loss of sensation (paralysis) usually signals a serious injury to the head or neck or other body area.

■ WHAT TO LOOK FOR—

- The athlete is unable to move his or her legs or body below a certain point.
- Tingling or numbness in the fingers and or toes.

■ WHAT TO DO—

CHECK the scene for safety. **CHECK** the injured athlete, following standard precautions when appropriate.
CALL 9-1-1 or the local emergency number.
CARE as for a head, neck or back injury:

1. Keep the athlete from moving, and immobilize the head and neck.
2. Check consciousness and breathing. If the athlete is not breathing, try to lift the chin without tilting the head back, pinch the nose and give 2 slow breaths.

3. Check for signs of circulation (normal breathing, coughing or movement in response to rescue breaths or a pulse) for no more than 10 seconds. Give rescue breathing (*see Rescue Breathing, p. 105*) or CPR (*p. 109*), as necessary.
4. Control any bleeding.
5. To minimize shock, keep the athlete from getting chilled or overheated.
6. *Do not move the athlete unless absolutely necessary.* If the athlete must be moved, do it carefully without twisting or bending the body. If alone, use the athlete's clothes to drag the athlete to safety while supporting the head and neck in the best way possible.

See also Cold-Related Emergencies (p. 167), Head, Neck or Back Injury (p. 135), Muscle, Bone and Joint (Musculoskeletal) Injuries (p. 147), and Sudden Illness (p. 165).

LYME DISEASE

(See Bites and Stings—Tick Bite, p. 86)

MOUTH AND JAW INJURY

A mouth injury may occur inside or outside the mouth. Bleeding may be heavy. As with any wound, the priority is to control bleeding with a sterile dressing and apply pressure on the wound.

■ WHAT TO DO—

CHECK the scene for safety. **CHECK** the injured athlete, following standard precautions when appropriate.
CALL 9-1-1 or the local emergency number if there are signals of a head, neck or back injury, changes in level of consciousness or breathing difficulty.

CARE:

If no serious head, neck or back injury is suspected—

1. Have the athlete lean slightly forward or place the athlete on his or her side.
2. Try to prevent the athlete from swallowing the blood, which may cause nausea or vomiting.
3. Apply the dressing:

For inside the cheek—
- Place folded sterile dressings inside the mouth against the wound.

For outside the cheek—
- Apply direct pressure using a sterile dressing.

For the tongue or lips—
- Apply direct pressure using a sterile dressing.
- Apply cold to reduce swelling and ease pain.

4. If teeth have been knocked out, *see also Teeth-Knocked Out (p. 176).*

If the injury to the mouth or cheek may be associated with a more serious head, neck or back injury—

5. Care for a head, neck or back injury (p. 135).
See also Wounds p. 179

▶ MOUTH TO STOMA BREATHING ◀

A person who has had part or all of the voice box removed breathes through a hole in the throat (called a stoma) instead of the mouth and nose. There may be visible scarring at the base of the neck. This person may wear medical alert identification.

Check for breathing at the stoma. When giving rescue breaths, breathe into the stoma in the same way you would give breaths at the mouth.

Moving an athlete may make some injuries worse. You should move an athlete only if there is immediate danger or the athlete has to be moved to give proper care. Even if you are in a remote area, such as when camping, it is often easier to bring professional medical help to the injured or ill athlete than move the athlete to the help. Once you decide to move someone, you must determine how to move them. Always consider your safety and the safety of the athlete. Use the appropriate technique for the situation:

- Clothes drag—used for an athlete with suspected head, neck, or back injury.

- Walking assist—used for a conscious athlete without suspected serious injury.

- Two-person seat carry—used for an athlete without suspected head, neck, or back injury.

Musculoskeletal

Usually only a trained medical professional can tell the difference between a sprain, strain, fracture, or dislocation. However, you do not need to know what kind of injury it is to provide the appropriate care. A fracture in which the skin is broken by the bone's broken end is an obvious fracture and serious emergency. The primary goal of care is to prevent further injury and get medical attention for the athlete.

■ WHAT TO LOOK FOR—

- Pain
- Bruising and swelling
- Obvious deformity
- Skin discoloration
- Inability to use the affected part normally
- Loss of sensation

■ WHAT TO DO—

CHECK the scene for safety. **CHECK** the injured athlete, following standard precautions as appropriate.

CALL 9-1-1 or the local emergency number for the following situations:

- Obvious deformity.
- Moderate or severe swelling and discoloration.
- Feels or sounds like bones are rubbing together.
- "Snap" or "pop" was heard or felt at the time of injury.
- A fracture with an open wound on or around the injury site (bone ends may or may not be visible).
- Inability to move or use the affected part normally.
- The injured area is cold and numb.
- The injury involves the head, neck or back.
- The injured athlete has breathing difficulty.
- The cause of the injury suggests that the injury may be severe.
- Not possible to safely or comfortably move athlete to vehicle for transport to a hospital.

CARE:

General care includes following "R.I.C.E."

1. **R**est—Avoid movement of the injured area.
2. **I**mmobilize—Splint the injured part if the athlete must be moved and it does not cause more pain.
3. **C**old—Apply ice to the injured area for about 20 minutes. Place a thin barrier between the ice and bare skin.
4. **E**levate—Elevate the injured part if it does not cause more pain.

Pelvic Injury

An injury to the pelvis may be serious or life threatening because of the risk of damage to major arteries or internal organs. Fracture of bones in this area may cause severe internal bleeding. The goals of first aid are to check for a potential serious injury, obtain immediate emergency medical care, and care for the athlete until EMS personnel arrive.

■ WHAT TO LOOK FOR—

- Severe pain
- Bruising
- Possible external bleeding
- Nausea
- Vomiting (vomit may include blood)
- Weakness
- Thirst
- Tenderness or a tight feeling in the abdomen
- Possible loss of sensation in the legs or inability to move the legs

■ WHAT TO DO—

CHECK the scene for safety. CHECK the injured athlete, following standard precautions when appropriate.
CALL 9-1-1 or the local emergency number.
CARE:

1. Do not move the athlete because of the possibility of a head, neck or back injury.

If organs are exposed in an open wound—

2. Keep the athlete lying flat if that position does not cause pain; otherwise keep the athlete in a comfortable position.

3. Remove any clothing from around the wound.
4. Do not apply pressure to organs or push them back inside.
5. Apply moist, sterile dressings or a clean cloth loosely over the wound.
6. Keep the dressing moist with warm water.
7. Place a sterile or clean cloth over the dressing to keep organs warm.
8. Give care to minimize shock (*p. 158*).

If organs are not exposed—

9. Keep the athlete lying flat if that position does not cause pain; otherwise keep the athlete in a comfortable position.
10. Give care to minimize shock (*p. 158*).

For care for possible head, neck or back injury, see p. 135.

▶ MUSCLE INJURY—CHARLEY HORSE ◀

A direct blow or muscle overuse may result in a painful condition known as a charley horse, a type of muscle strain or bruise.

■ WHAT TO LOOK FOR—

- Localized pain
- Swelling
- Loss of motion in the muscle

■ WHAT TO DO—

CHECK the scene for safety. **CHECK** the injured athlete, following standard precautions when appropriate.
CALL 9-1-1 or the local emergency number if there are signals of a serious injury.
CARE:

1. Care for any more serious injuries suspected, such as bone or joint injury (*p. 147*).

For a charley horse (in the absence of a more serious injury)—

2. Apply ice 20 minutes on, 20 minutes off.
3. Apply an elastic bandage above, over, and below the area, without leaving an opening for swelling to develop or blood to pool. (*See Bandaging, p. 77*)
4. Stretch slowly while icing.
5. Do not apply heat (in the first 48 hours).
6. Do not bounce on the affected leg.
7. Do not continue athletic activity while signals persist.

See also Muscle, Bone and Joint (Musculoskeletal) Injuries, (p. 147).

▶ MUSCLE INJURY—CRAMPS ◀

A muscle cramp is a sudden muscle contraction resulting from overuse, heat- or cold-related, usually occurring in the arm, foot or calf. Such an injury is serious only if it puts the athlete in a life-threatening situation, such as a swimmer who is unable to reach safety after a cramp occurs. A cramp of abdominal muscles may be mistakenly called a stomach cramp. A heat cramp is a muscle cramp that results from overheating.

■ WHAT TO LOOK FOR—

- Immediate tightness and spasm in the muscle
- Pain

■ WHAT TO DO—

CHECK the scene for safety. **CHECK** the injured athlete, following standard precautions as appropriate.

CALL 9-1-1 or the local emergency number if there are any signals of a serious condition.

CARE:

1. Have the athlete stop activity; a swimmer should leave the water.
2. Lightly stretch the affected area immediately; for a leg cramp, extend the leg and flex the ankle.
3. Massage the area of muscle where the spasm is occurring.
4. For an abdominal cramp, help the athlete get comfortable and rest. Ensure the cramp was caused by exertion or cold water, not by a possible internal injury (*p. 141*) or sudden illness (*p. 165*).
5. For muscle cramps related to being overheated, have the athlete rest in a cool place and give cool water or a commercial sports drink. Watch for the signals of heat-related emergencies (p. 171) and send someone to call EMS personnel if necessary.

See also Muscle, Bone and Joint (Musculoskeletal) Injuries, (p. 147).

▶ MUSCLE INJURY—PULLED MUSCLE ◀

A pulled muscle is a type of muscle strain, which is a stretching and tearing of muscles or tendons. It may result from improper stretching, muscular overuse, or a sudden twisting motion.

■ WHAT TO LOOK FOR—

- Pain
- Tightness in muscle
- Swelling
- Occasional loss of motion if severe

■ WHAT TO DO—

CHECK the scene for safety. **CHECK** the injured athlete, following standard precautions as appropriate.

CALL 9-1-1 or the local emergency number if there are any signals of a serious condition.

CARE:

1. Apply ice 20 minutes on, 20 minutes off.
2. Wrap the area with an elastic bandage.
3. Seek medical advice before resuming athletic activities.
4. Be careful not to assume a possibly serious injury is only a pulled muscle. Any injury involving bones or joints may be more serious.

See also Muscle, Bone and Joint Injuries (p. 147).

► NAUSEA—SUDDEN ILLNESS ◄

Nausea without an obvious cause may be a signal of a serious condition. Check for other signals. If the athlete's nausea is without explanation or is especially severe or if the athlete has other signals, the goals of first aid are to check the athlete for the problems listed here and care for any problem found.

- Head, Neck or Back Injury (*p. 135*)
- Heat-Related Emergencies (*p. 171*)
- Internal Injury (*p. 141*)
- Poisoning (*p. 155*)
- Sudden Illness (*p. 165*)

■ WHAT TO DO—

CHECK the scene for safety. **CHECK** the athlete, follow standard precautions when appropriate.

CALL 9-1-1 or the local emergency number if there are signals of a serious condition.

CARE:

1. Be prepared to give care for vomiting (*p. 178*).
2. Care for specific problems found, and care for sudden illness (*p. 165*).

(See Wounds—Nosebleed, p. 190)

PARALYSIS

(See Loss of Sensation, p. 143)

PELVIC INJURY

(See Muscle, Bone and Joint Injuries—Pelvic Injury, p. 149)

PLANTS—POISONOUS

Poison ivy, poison oak and poison sumac are the most common poisonous plants. Some athletes are allergic to these plants and have dramatic reactions after contact, while others may not even have a rash.

■ WHAT TO LOOK FOR—

- Itching
- Red rash, often progressing to weeping sores
- Swelling

■ WHAT TO DO—

CHECK the scene for safety. **CHECK** the athlete, follow standard precautions.
CALL 9-1-1 or the local emergency number if there are signals of a serious condition.
CARE:
1. Immediately wash the affected area thoroughly with soap and water.
2. If a rash or open sores develop, apply a paste of baking soda and water several times a day to reduce discomfort.
3. Lotions, such as calamine or Caladryl®, may help

soothe the area. Antihistamines, such as Benadryl®, may also help dry up the sores.

4. If the condition worsens or affects large areas of the body or face, seek medical attention.

Poison Ivy

Ken Samuelsen/Getty Images

Poison Oak

Jeri Gleiter/Taxi/Getty Images

Poison Sumac

Larry West/Taxi/Getty Images

POISONING

A poison is a substance that causes injury or illness if it enters the body. There are four ways a poison may enter the body—by swallowing it, breathing it, touching it or having it injected.

Combinations of certain substances, such as drugs and alcohol, may be poisonous, although if taken by themselves they might not cause harm. Not everyone reacts to poisons in the same way. A substance that is harmful to one may not always be harmful to another.

Many poisonings can be cared for without the help of EMS personnel. Poison Control Center (PCC) personnel have access to information on most poisonous substances and can tell you what care to give to counteract the poison. Keep the PCC telephone number (800) 222-1222, posted by the telephone. Also record it on the form on page 62 of this guide.

■ WHAT TO LOOK FOR—

- Breathing difficulty
- Nausea, vomiting, diarrhea
- Chest or abdominal pain
- Sweating, changes in consciousness, seizure
- Headache
- Dizziness
- Irregular pupil size
- Burning/tearing of the eyes
- Abnormal skin color
- Burns around the lips, tongue or on the skin
- Open or spilled containers
- Unusual odors, flames, smoke
- Unusual behavior suggesting drug use

Allergic reactions are also a type of poisoning and may be life threatening (p. 73).

■ WHAT TO DO—

CHECK the scene to make sure it is safe to approach. CHECK the athlete, follow standard precautions when appropriate.

- Gather clues about what happened.
- Follow standard precautions to avoid contact with poison or body fluids.

- Look for any containers and have the caller take them to the telephone.
- If you suspect someone has swallowed a poison, try to find out what type of poison it was, how much was taken and when it was taken.

CALL the Poison Control Center at (800) 222-1222. If the athlete is unconscious or if another life-threatening condition is present, call 9-1-1 or the local emergency number.

CARE:
1. If necessary, move the athlete to safety, away from the source of the poison.
2. Check the athlete's level of consciousness, breathing and signs of circulation (normal breathing, coughing or movement in response to rescue breaths or a pulse).
3. Care for any life-threatening conditions first.
4. Never give anything to eat or drink unless directed to do so by the Poison Control Center or a medical professional.
5. If the athlete vomits, position the athlete on his or her side. Save a sample of the vomit if the poison is not known so that the poison can be identified if necessary.

Note: In cases of poisoning by a substance in contact with the skin, wash the area thoroughly with running water (see Burns—Chemical, p. 98).

PUNCTURE WOUND

(See Wounds—Puncture, p. 191)

RASH

(See Allergic Reactions, p. 73)

RECOVERY POSITION

(See Checking an Unconscious Athlete—Adult or Child, p. 105)

RESCUE BREATHING—ADULT OR CHILD ATHLETE

(See Checking an Unconscious Athlete—Rescue Breathing—Adult or Child, p. 105)

SCORPION STING

(See Bites and Stings—Scorpion Sting, p. 83)

SCRAPES

(See Wounds—Abrasions, p. 181)

SEIZURE

(See Sudden Illness—Seizure, p. 172)

SEVERED BODY PART

(See Wounds—Amputation/Avulsion p. 182)

SHOCK

Shock is a life-threatening condition in which not enough blood is being delivered to all parts of the body. Body organs begin to fail. Shock may be caused by severe bleeding, serious internal injury, significant fluid loss or other conditions. An athlete going into shock needs immediate medical attention. The goals of first aid are to obtain help quickly and give care to minimize shock while caring for the injury or illness.

■ WHAT TO LOOK FOR—
- Restlessness or irritability
- Altered consciousness

- Pale or ashen, cool, moist skin
- Rapid breathing
- Rapid pulse
- Excessive thirst
- Nausea or vomiting

■ WHAT TO DO—

CHECK the scene for safety. **CHECK** the injured athlete, following standard precautions when appropriate.
CALL 9-1-1 or the local emergency number.
CARE:

1. Have the athlete lie down and rest comfortably (pain worsens shock).
2. Control any external bleeding (*see Wounds—Bleeding, p. 182*).
3. Keep the athlete from getting chilled or overheated.
4. Reassure the athlete (anxiety may worsen shock).
5. Unless you suspect a head, neck or back injury or broken bones in the hips or legs, elevate the legs about 12 inches.
6. Do not give anything to drink or eat, even though the athlete may ask for it.

See also Wounds—Bleeding (p. 182), Internal Injury (p. 141), and Sudden Illness—Fainting (p. 170).

▶ SMOKE INHALATION ◀

Smoke inhalation may injure respiratory passages or the lungs, affecting breathing and the oxygenation of blood. It may be life threatening.

■ WHAT TO LOOK FOR—

- Breathing difficulty
- Coughing
- Burns, ash, or soot about the nose or mouth

■ WHAT TO DO—

CHECK the scene for safety. **CHECK** the injured athlete, following standard precautions when appropriate.

CALL 9-1-1 or the local emergency number.

CARE:

1. Move the athlete to fresh air.
2. CHECK breathing and circulation.

If the athlete is conscious—

3. Support the athlete in the position in which it is easiest to breathe and monitor breathing.

If the athlete is unconscious—

4. Place the athlete on his or her side and monitor breathing closely (p. 105).

See also Burns (p. 94) and Breathing Difficulty (p. 88).

▶ SNAKE BITE ◀

(See Bites and Stings—Snake Bite, p. 84)

▶ SPIDER BITE ◀

(See Bites and Stings—Spider Bite, p. 85)

▶ SPINAL INJURY ◀

(See Head, Neck or Back Injury, p. 135)

▶ SPLINTING ◀

(See Muscle, Bone and Joint [Musculoskeletal] Injuries, p. 147)

Splinting is a method of immobilizing an injured body part to keep it from moving. It may also help to reduce pain, making the injured athlete more comfortable. Splint *only* if the athlete must be moved or transported and if you can do so without causing more pain and discomfort to the athlete. Immobilization may be used when appropriate for any musculoskeletal injury, including fractures, dislocations, sprains and joint injuries. You do not need to know the specific type of injury before deciding to splint it.

Immobilization guidelines
- Immobilize an injury in the position you find it.
- Immobilize the joints above and below an injured bone.
- Immobilize the bones above and below an injured joint.
- Check for warmth and color of the skin below the site of the injury both before and after splinting.

Methods
There are a variety of ways to immobilize an injured body part. Choose a method using materials at hand that will best keep the injured part from moving. Simply supporting the injured part in the position you find it, such as placing a small pillow or folded blanket under an injured leg against the ground, is the best method of all.

Anatomic splint
A part of the body used to immobilize the injured part (an injured leg can be splinted to an uninjured leg).

Soft splint

Made with soft materials, such as folded blankets, towels or pillows.

Sling

A triangular bandage tied to support an injured arm, wrist or hand.

Rigid splint

Made with boards, folded magazines, or newspaper strips.

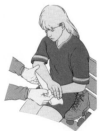 

See also Muscle, Bone and Joint Injuries (p. 147).

SPRAINS

(See Muscle, Bone and Joint [Musculoskeletal] Injuries, p. 147)

STINGRAY STING

(See Bites and Stings—Marine Life Sting, p. 82)

STINGS

(See Bites and Stings, pp. 79-88)

STOMA

(See Mouth to Stoma Breathing, p. 108)

STRAINS

(See Muscle, Bone and Joint [Musculoskeletal] Injuries, p. 147)

STROKE

(See Sudden Illness—Stroke, p. 174)

SUBSTANCE ABUSE

A wide range of drugs and other substances are abused in our society, with a wide range of psychological and physical effects. Your goal is not to try to diagnose a clear case of the athlete being under the influence of a drug or other substance. The goal of care is to recognize a possible overdose or other problem requiring medical attention or other professional help. Do not be judgmental or assume an illegal drug is involved. Instead, treat the situation like any other case of sudden illness (*p. 165*).

■ WHAT TO LOOK FOR—

- Behavioral changes not otherwise explained
- Sudden mood changes
- Restlessness, talkativeness, irritability
- Altered consciousness
- Slurred speech, poor coordination
- Moist or flushed skin
- Chills, nausea, vomiting
- Dizziness, confusion
- Irregular pulse
- Irregular breathing
- Loss of consciousness

■ WHAT TO DO—

CHECK the scene for safety. **CHECK** the injured athlete, following standard precautions as appropriate.

CALL the Poison Control Center (800-222-1222) and follow their directions if you have good reason to suspect a substance was taken. **CALL** 9-1-1 or the local emergency number if—

- The athlete is unconscious, confused, or seems to be losing consciousness.
- The athlete has breathing difficulty or is breathing irregularly.
- The athlete has persistent chest pain or pressure.
- The athlete has pressure or pain in the abdomen that does not go away.
- The athlete is vomiting blood or passing blood.
- The athlete has a seizure, severe headache or slurred speech.

- The athlete engages in violent behavior.
- You are unsure what to do.
- You are unsure about the severity of the problem.

CARE:
1. Try to learn from others what substance may have been taken.
2. Calm and reassure the athlete.
3. To minimize shock, keep the athlete from getting chilled or overheated.

See also Poisoning p. 155 and Sudden Illness (below).

SUDDEN ILLNESS

Many different types of sudden illness often have similar signals. Usually you will not know the exact cause of the illness, but this should not keep you from providing care. Care for the signals you find.

■ WHAT TO LOOK FOR—
- Feeling lightheaded, dizzy, confused or weak
- Changes in skin color (pale, ashen or flushed skin), sweating
- Nausea, vomiting or diarrhea

Some illnesses may also include the following:
- Seizure or changes in consciousness;
- Paralysis (inability to move), slurred speech, or blurred vision; or
- Severe headache, breathing difficulty, persistent pressure or pain.

■ WHAT TO DO—
CHECK the scene for safety. **CHECK** the injured athlete, following standard precautions as appropriate.

CALL 9-1-1 or the local emergency number for the following situations:

- The athlete is unconscious, confused or seems to be losing consciousness.
- The athlete has breathing difficulty or is breathing irregularly.
- The athlete has persistent chest pain or pressure.
- The athlete has pressure or pain in the abdomen that does not go away.
- The athlete is vomiting blood or passing blood.
- The athlete has a seizure, severe headache or slurred speech.
- The athlete appears to have been poisoned.
- The athlete has injuries to the head, neck or back.
- You are unsure how to handle the problem.
- You are unsure about the severity of the illness.

CARE:

1. Check for the signals of an allergic reaction, such as breathing difficulty, a feeling of tightness in the chest and throat and swelling of the face, neck, and tongue.
2. Care for any life-threatening conditions first.
3. Help the athlete rest comfortably.
4. To minimize shock, keep the athlete from getting chilled or overheated.
5. Reassure the athlete.
6. Watch for changes in consciousness, breathing and circulation.
7. Do not give anything to eat or drink unless the athlete is fully conscious.
8. Care for any problems that develop, such as *vomiting* (*p. 178*), *unconsciousness* (*p. 103*) or *stopped breathing* (*p. 105*).

See also Sudden Illness—Diabetic Emergency (p. 168), Sudden Illness—Seizure (p. 172) and Sudden Illness—Stroke (p. 174).

Hypothermia and frostbite are cold-related emergencies. Both conditions may quickly become life or limb threatening. Frostbite is the freezing of body parts (*p. 134*). Hypothermia is the cooling of the body caused by the failure of the body's warming system (*p. 27*). The goals of first aid are to restore normal body temperature and to care for any conditions while waiting for EMS personnel.

■ HOW TO PREVENT—

Preventing cold-related emergencies includes not starting an activity in, on, or around cold water unless you know you can get help quickly in an emergency. Be aware of the wind chill.

Dress appropriately and avoid staying in the cold too long. Wear a hat and gloves when appropriate with layers of clothing. Drink plenty of warm fluids or warm water but *avoid* caffeine and alcohol.

Stay active to maintain body heat. Take frequent breaks from the cold. Avoid unnecessary exposure of any part of the body to the cold. Get out of the cold immediately if the signals of hypothermia or frostbite appear.

■ WHAT TO LOOK FOR—

Signals of hypothermia—
- Shivering, numbness, glassy stare
- Apathy, weakness, impaired judgment
- Loss of consciousness

Signals of frostbite—
- Lack of feeling in an affected area
- Skin that appears waxy, cold to the touch or discolored (flushed, white, yellow or blue)

■ WHAT TO DO—

CHECK the scene for safety. **CHECK** the injured athlete, following standard precautions when appropriate.

CALL 9-1-1 or the local emergency number.

CARE:

1. Gently move the athlete to a warm place.
2. Monitor breathing and circulation.
3. Give rescue breathing (*see Rescue Breathing, p. 105*) and CPR (*p. 109*) if needed.
4. Remove any wet clothing and dry the athlete.
5. Warm the athlete slowly by wrapping in blankets or by putting dry clothing on the athlete. Hot water bottles and chemical hot packs may be used when first wrapped in a towel or blanket before applying.

Do not warm the athlete too quickly, such as by immersing him or her in warm water. Rapid warming may cause dangerous heart rhythms.

See Frostbite (p. 134).

▶ SUDDEN ILLNESS—DIABETIC EMERGENCY ◀

Diabetes is a condition in which the body is unable to balance insulin and sugar levels in the body. You will not be able to tell what the body needs. Giving sugar will not cause additional harm.

You may know that the athlete is diabetic, or you may see a medical alert bracelet. If there is no evidence that the athlete is diabetic, then give care as for sudden illness (*p. 165*).

■ WHAT TO LOOK FOR—

- Medical alert bracelet or tag
- Feeling lightheaded, dizzy, confused or weak
- Irregular breathing
- Irregular pulse
- Feeling or looking ill
- May become unconscious

■ WHAT TO DO—

CHECK the scene for safety. **CHECK** the injured athlete, following standard precautions as appropriate.

CALL 9-1-1 or the local emergency number if there are any signals of a serious condition.

CARE:

1. If the athlete is conscious and a known diabetic, give sugar (glucose paste or tablets, fruit juices, candy, non-diet soft drinks, table sugar).
2. If the athlete is not feeling better in about 5 minutes, send someone to call EMS personnel.

If the athlete becomes unconscious—

3. Send someone to call 9-1-1 or the local emergency number if you have not done so already.
4. Check signs of circulation and care for the conditions you find.

See Rescue Breathing (p. 105) and CPR (p. 109).

5. Do not give anything to eat or drink.

See also Sudden Illness (p. 165).

▶ SUDDEN ILLNESS—DIARRHEA ◀

■ WHAT TO DO—

CHECK the scene for safety. **CHECK** the injured athlete, following standard precautions when appropriate.

CALL 9-1-1 or the local emergency number if you suspect a more serious condition.

CARE:

Ongoing diarrhea may indicate a serious condition. If its onset is sudden and without explanation, look for other signals, consider the following problems as possible causes, and give appropriate care.

- Poisoning (p. 155)
- Sudden illness (p. 165)

Severe diarrhea may cause a dangerous loss of body fluid, which may lead to shock and other serious problems (*p. 158*). Therefore, this condition should be considered potentially serious.

Coaches should be sensitive to an athlete with this condition.

▶ SUDDEN ILLNESS—FAINTING ◀

Fainting is a temporary loss of consciousness. It may be a signal of a more serious condition. The goals of care are to determine if emergency care is needed and care for the athlete until EMS personnel arrive.

■ WHAT TO DO—

CHECK the scene for safety. **CHECK** the injured athlete, following standard precautions when appropriate.
CALL 9-1-1 or the local emergency number if you suspect a more serious condition.
CARE:
1. Check breathing and signs of circulation (coughing or movement in response to rescue breaths or a pulse).
2. Elevate the legs about 8 to 12 inches if injury is not suspected.
3. Loosen any tight clothing.
4. Do not give the athlete anything to eat or drink.

Feeling faint may be a signal of a number of serious conditions, such as the following. Look for additional signals that suggest any of these conditions, and give the care described. If you find no other signals, give care for *sudden illness* (*p. 165*).
- Allergic Reactions (*p. 72*)
- Head, Neck or Back Injury (*p. 135*)
- Chest Pain or Pressure (*p. 123*)
- Sudden Illness—Cold-Related Emergencies (*p. 167*)
- Burns—Electrical (*p. 99*)
- Heat-Related Emergencies (*p. 171*)

- Poisoning (*p. 155*)
- Shock (*p. 158*)
- Substance Abuse (*p. 163*)
- Sudden Illness—Diabetic Emergency (*p. 168*)

SUDDEN ILLNESS—HEAT RELATED

Heat-related emergencies are progressive conditions caused by overexposure to heat. If recognized in the early stages, heat-related emergencies can usually be reversed. If not, they may progress to heat stroke, a life-threatening condition.

■ HOW TO PREVENT—

Prevention strategies include scheduling practice during cooler times of the day and using proper equipment. When appropriate, athletes should wear net-type jerseys or wear light-weight, light-colored, cotton T-shirts and shorts. Be certain athletes are fully hydrated before practice and competition. Schedule and enforce frequent water breaks. **Do not** use salt tablets.

Reduce or cancel practice when the weather is excessively hot or humid. When athletes are practicing or competing, allow time for adjustment to warmer climates.

■ WHAT TO LOOK FOR—

Early stages (sometimes called heat exhaustion)

- Cool, moist, pale, ashen or flushed skin
- Headache, nausea, dizziness
- Weakness, exhaustion
- Heavy sweating

Late stages (sometimes called heat stroke)

- Red, hot, dry skin
- Changes in level of consciousness
- Vomiting

■ WHAT TO DO—

CHECK the scene for safety. **CHECK** the athlete, follow standard precautions when appropriate.

CALL 9-1-1 or the local emergency number if the situation warrants.

CARE:

1. Move the athlete to a cool place.
2. Loosen tight clothing.
3. Remove perspiration-soaked clothing.
4. Apply cool, wet cloths to the skin.
5. Fan the athlete.
6. If conscious, give small amounts of cool water to drink.

If the athlete refuses water, vomits or starts to lose consciousness

1. Send someone to call EMS personnel.
2. Place the athlete on his or her side.
3. Continue to cool the athlete by using ice or cold packs on the wrists, ankles, groin, and neck and in the armpits.
4. Continue to check breathing and signs of circulation (coughing or movement in response to rescue breaths or a pulse).

See also Muscle Injury—Cramps (p. 151).

▶ SUDDEN ILLNESS—SEIZURE ◀

A seizure is a loss of body control that occurs when brain functions are disrupted by injury or illness. Seizure disorders include epilepsy and can usually be controlled by medication, although the athlete may still have occasional seizures. The goals for care are to protect the athlete from injury during the seizure, ensure that the airway stays open, and call EMS personnel when appropriate.

■ WHAT TO LOOK FOR—

- Mild seizure may be a short, temporary blackout.
- Major seizure may be sudden, uncontrolled muscular contractions (convulsions) of part of or the entire body.
- The athlete may have an unusual sensation (aura) before the seizure occurs.
- Presence of medical alert tag or bracelet for seizure disorder.

■ WHAT TO DO—

CHECK the scene for safety. **CHECK** the injured athlete, following standard precautions when appropriate.

CALL 9-1-1 or the local emergency number *unless* you know the athlete has a seizure disorder or epilepsy. Even if the athlete has epilepsy, call EMS personnel if—

- The seizure lasts longer than a few minutes or is repeated.
- The athlete does not regain consciousness.
- The athlete is pregnant, known to be a diabetic or is injured.

CARE:

1. Remove nearby objects that might cause injury.
2. Protect the athlete's head by placing a folded towel or clothing beneath it.
3. Do not hold or restrain the athlete.
4. Do not place anything between the athlete's teeth.
5. Place the athlete on the side to drain fluids from his or her mouth.
6. When the seizure is over, check for breathing and other injuries. If necessary, perform rescue breathing (*see Rescue Breathing, p. 105*) or CPR (*Checking An Unconscious Athlete-CPR p. 109*).
7. Reassure and comfort the athlete.

8. Stay with the athlete until he or she is fully conscious, oriented to the surroundings, and able to care for himself or herself.

See also Sudden Illness, (p. 165).

SUDDEN ILLNESS—STROKE

A stroke is a disruption of blood flow to a part of the brain serious enough to damage brain tissue, often resulting when a blood vessel bursts or becomes narrowed by a clot. Stroke may also result from a head injury, high blood pressure, or other conditions. The goals of care are to get emergency medical help quickly and prevent further problems while waiting for EMS personnel to arrive.

■ WHAT TO LOOK FOR—

- Looking or feeling ill
- *Sudden* weakness and numbness of the face, arm or leg, usually on one side
- *Sudden* difficulty talking
- *Sudden* difficulty understanding speech
- *Sudden* blurred or dimmed vision
- Unequal pupil size
- *Sudden* severe headache
- Dizziness, confusion
- Ringing in the ears
- Loss of bladder or bowel control
- Loss of consciousness

■ WHAT TO DO—

CHECK the scene for safety. **CHECK** the injured athlete, following standard precautions when appropriate.
CALL 9-1-1 or the local emergency number *immediately*.

CARE:
1. Care for the specific conditions you find. Keep the airway open if the athlete becomes unconscious.
2. If the athlete is drooling or having difficulty swallowing, place on his or her side to keep the airway clear *(p. 105)*.
3. Try to reassure the athlete.
4. Help the athlete rest in a comfortable position.
5. Do not give the athlete anything to eat or drink.

See also Sudden Illness (p. 165).

SUNBURN

(See Burns—Sunburn, p. 100)

SWEATING—UNUSUAL

Sweating without an appropriate obvious cause (exertion or exercise) may be a signal of a serious condition. Check for other signals. If the athlete is sweating unusually heavily or if the athlete has other signals, consider the conditions listed here and give care for the appropriate problem. Otherwise, provide the care for *sudden illness (p. 165)*.

- Breathing Difficulty *(p. 88)*
- Chest Pain or Pressure *(p. 123)*
- Heat-Related Emergencies *(p. 171)*
- Internal Injury *(p. 141)*
- Poisoning *(p. 155)*
- Shock *(p. 158)*
- Substance Abuse *(p. 163)*

SWELLING

Swelling is a common signal of musculoskeletal injuries. *See Muscle, Bone and Joint (Musculoskeletal) Injuries, p. 147.*

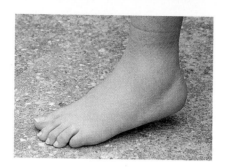

Swelling of a body area may also result from abdominal injury (p. 69), the bite or sting of an insect or animal (*pp. 78-88*), a burn (p. 94), exposure to a poisonous plant (p. 154), such as poison ivy or internal injury (*p. 141*).

Swelling of the face and mouth, and in particular the tissues of the airway, typically signals an allergic reaction (*p. 72*). In any instance of an allergic reaction, call 9-1-1 or the local emergency number immediately.

▶ TEETH—KNOCKED OUT ◀

Teeth may be knocked out in any injury involving the mouth or head. The goals of care are to check for any additional serious injury, care for the bleeding inside the mouth and preserve the tooth for possible re-implantation.

■ WHAT TO DO—

CHECK the scene for safety. **CHECK** the injured athlete, following standard precautions.
CALL 9-1-1 or the local emergency number if there are signals of a serious condition.
CARE:
1. Have the athlete bite down on a rolled sterile dressing in the space left by the tooth (or teeth).

2. Save any displaced teeth:
   - Carefully pick up the tooth by the crown (white part), *not* the root.
   - Rinse off the root of the tooth in water if it's dirty. *Do not* scrub it or remove any attached tissue fragments.
   - Place the tooth in milk, if possible, or water and take it with you.
3. Get the athlete to a dentist as soon as possible.
4. If the athlete's tooth was knocked out by significant impact, also evaluate the athlete for a head, neck or back injury (*p. 135*).

See also Mouth and Jaw Injury, (p. 144), Wounds (p. 179), and Head, Neck or Back Injury (p. 135).

TICK BITE

(See Bites and Stings—Tick Bite, p. 86)

TRANSPORTING AN INJURED ATHLETE

Some musculoskeletal injuries are obviously minor and do not require professional medical care. Others are obviously more serious and may require you to call EMS personnel. If you discover a life-threatening emergency or think it likely for one to develop, send someone to call EMS personnel and wait for help. Always call EMS personnel for any injury involving the following:

- Severe bleeding
- Injuries to the head, neck or back
- Possible broken bones that may be difficult to transport properly, such as the hip and legs

Fractures of large bones may bleed internally or externally and are likely to cause shock (p. 158). Do not attempt to transport an athlete with such an injury.

Some injuries are not serious enough for you to call EMS personnel but may still require professional medical care. If you decide to transport the injured athlete yourself to a medical facility, follow the general rule: When in doubt, splint.

Always splint the injury before moving the athlete. If possible, have someone drive you so you can continue to provide care.

See also Moving an Injured Athlete (p. 146).

▶ VOMITING ◀

Vomiting without an obvious cause may be a signal of a serious condition. Check for other signals. If the athlete's vomiting is without explanation or is especially severe or if the athlete has other signals, consider the problems listed here and give the appropriate care:

- Head, Neck or Back Injury (p. 135)
- Heat-Related Emergencies (p. 171)
- Internal Injury (p. 141)
- Poisoning (p. 155)
- Sudden Illness (p. 165)

■ WHAT TO DO—

CHECK the scene for safety. **CHECK** the injured athlete, following standard precautions as appropriate.

CALL 9-1-1 or the local emergency number for any athlete who vomits blood or an athlete with possible heat stroke who vomits.

CARE:

1. Keep the airway open.
2. Turn an unconscious breathing athlete on the side to let the mouth drain (*p. 105*).
3. Wipe the mouth clean.
4. Give additional care as needed.

► WASP STING ◄

(See Bites and Stings—Bee Sting, p. 79)

► WATER RESCUE METHODS ◄

(See Drowning/Near-Drowning, p. 130)

► WOUNDS ◄

A wound is an injury to the skin and underlying soft tissues. Damage to blood vessels causes bleeding. When caring for wounds, the goals of care are to control bleeding, prevent infection and minimize shock.

■ WHAT TO LOOK FOR—

- Cuts, scrapes, punctures or other breaks in the skin
- Bleeding
- Bruising
- Swelling

■ WHAT TO DO—

CHECK the scene for safety. **CHECK** the injured athlete, following standard precautions. Wash hands thoroughly after giving care.

CALL 9-1-1 or the local emergency number for the following situations:

- Bleeding that cannot be stopped
- Wounds that show muscle or bone, involve joints, gape widely or involve hands or feet
- Large or deep wounds
- Large or deeply embedded objects in the wound (Do not remove embedded objects.)
- Human or animal bites
- Any wound that would leave an obvious scar, such as on the face
- Skin or body parts that have been partially or completely torn away

CARE:

1. Cover the wound with a sterile gauze pad and press firmly against the wound. (Use your bare hand to apply pressure only as a last resort.)
2. If bleeding continues, use pressure, elevation and bandaging to control the bleeding. Add more dressings as needed. For complete care, see *Wounds—Bleeding* (*p. 182*).
3. In cases of serious bleeding, shock is likely; give care to minimize shock (*p. 159*).
4. If the wound was caused by an object that could carry infection, check with a doctor whether a tetanus booster may be needed.

See also Wounds—Abrasions (below), Wounds—Amputation/Avulsion (p. 182), Wounds—Embedded Object (p. 188), and Wounds—Puncture (p. 191).

▶ WOUNDS—ABRASIONS ◀

An abrasion is a type of wound in which the skin has been rubbed or scraped away. An important goal of care is to prevent infection, as dirt or other foreign matter is often ground into the wound.

■ WHAT TO LOOK FOR—
- Raw, red area
- Minimal bleeding (may be oozing)
- Pain

■ WHAT TO DO—
CHECK the scene for safety. **CHECK** the injured athlete, following standard precautions when appropriate.
CALL 9-1-1 or the local emergency number if there are signals of any serious condition.
CARE:
1. Wash the wound with soap and warm water.
2. Place a sterile dressing over the wound.
3. Apply direct pressure for a few minutes if needed to control bleeding.
4. When bleeding is controlled, remove the dressing and apply an antibiotic ointment.
5. Apply a new dressing and bandage.

If the abrasion was caused by an object that may carry infection—

Check with a doctor whether a tetanus booster may be necessary.

If bleeding does not stop immediately—

Give additional care to stop bleeding: elevate the limb and maintain pressure with a bandage. *See Wounds—Bleeding, p. 182.*

► WOUNDS—AMPUTATION/AVULSION ◄

Amputation or an avulsion is a wound in which a part of the body has been torn or cut off. The goals of first aid are to care for the wound and maintain the severed body part for potential surgical reattachment.

■ WHAT TO DO—

CHECK the scene for safety. **CHECK** the injured athlete, following standard precautions when appropriate.
CALL 9-1-1 or the local emergency number.
CARE:
1. Control bleeding (*see below*).
2. Wrap and bandage the wound to prevent infection.
3. If bleeding is significant, give care to minimize shock (*p. 159*).
4. Wrap the severed body part in sterile gauze or a clean cloth.
5. Place the severed body part in a plastic bag.
6. Put the plastic bag on ice (but do not freeze it) and keep it with the athlete.

See also Wounds (p. 180).

▶ WOUNDS—BLEEDING ◀

Any serious bleeding may rapidly become life threatening. The goal of care is to control it as quickly as possible in a way that helps protect both the athlete and you from infection.

For internal bleeding (inside the body), see Internal Injury (*p. 141*).

■ WHAT TO DO—

CHECK the scene for safety. **CHECK** the injured athlete, following standard precautions.
CALL 9-1-1 or the local emergency number for:
- Bleeding that cannot be stopped;
- Wounds that show muscle or bone;
- Wounds that involve joints;

- Wounds that gape widely;
- Serious wounds that involve hands or feet;
- Large or deep wounds;
- Large or deeply embedded objects in the wound;
- Human or animal bites;
- Any wound that would leave an obvious scar, such as on the face; or
- Skin or body parts that have been partially or completely torn away (*see Wounds-Amputation/Avulsion, p. 181*).

CARE:

1. Cover the wound with a sterile gauze pad and press firmly. (Only use your bare hand to apply pressure as a last resort.)
2. Elevate the injured area above the level of the heart if you do not suspect broken bones.

3. Cover gauze dressings with a roller bandage to maintain pressure.

4. If the dressing becomes soaked with blood, do not remove it. Apply additional dressings and bandages on top.

5. Squeeze the nearby artery against the bone underneath the artery:

- Arm: Inside of the upper arm, between the shoulder and elbow; or
- Leg: Crease at the front of the hip, in the groin

6. Minimize shock, which is likely in an athlete with serious bleeding (*p. 159*).

See also Bandaging (p. 75) and Wounds (p. 179).

A bruise is caused by bleeding under the skin resulting from damage to blood vessels or soft tissues. A bruise may signal an internal serious injury.

■ WHAT TO LOOK FOR—

- Discoloration (often red first, then purple or dark red)
- Pain
- Possible swelling

■ WHAT TO DO—

CHECK the scene for safety. **CHECK** the injured athlete, following standard precautions as appropriate.
CALL 9-1-1 or the local emergency number if signals of a serious injury are present.
CARE:

For bruises not associated with a serious injury—

1. Apply ice or a cold pack to help control pain and swelling. To prevent further injury, place a towel or cloth between the ice or cold pack and the skin.
2. Elevate the injured part to reduce swelling.

If a serious injury may be present—

3. *Check for signals of internal injury (p. 141),* head, neck or back injury *(p. 135).*
4. Give care for any additional serious conditions found.
See also Muscle, Bone and Joint (Musculoskeletal) Injuries (p. 147).

A chest injury may be an open, bleeding wound or a closed wound with internal injury. A chest wound may be life threatening because of internal or external bleeding, broken bones, injury to internal organs, and breathing difficulty. The goals of first aid are to care for life-threatening conditions and call EMS personnel.

■ WHAT TO LOOK FOR—

- Obvious wound or deformity of chest area
- Severe pain
- Breathing difficulty
- Flushed, pale, ashen or bluish discoloration of skin (signals of shock)
- Bruising at the site
- Coughing up blood
- Sucking or burping noise during breathing

■ WHAT TO DO—

CHECK the scene for safety. **CHECK** the injured athlete, following standard precautions as appropriate.
CALL 9-1-1 or the local emergency number.
CARE:
1. Keep the athlete from moving and in a comfortable position for breathing.
2. Cover the wound with a sterile dressing or clean cloth and bandage in place.
3. Watch for changes in the athlete's condition.
4. If bubbles are forming around the wound, cover it with plastic wrap or material that does not allow air to pass through. Tape the dressing in place, leaving one corner open to allow air to escape when the athlete exhales.

► WOUNDS—EAR INJURY ◄

Ear injuries include internal injury, such as a rupture of the eardrum from a sudden blow to the head, external injuries and foreign objects lodged in the ear.

■ WHAT TO LOOK FOR—

- Blood or fluid draining from the ear
- Pain
- Loss of hearing

■ WHAT TO DO—

CHECK the scene for safety. **CHECK** the injured athlete, following standard precautions.

CALL 9-1-1 or the local emergency number if blood or other fluid is draining from the ear or the situation otherwise warrants it.

CARE:

If there is blood or other fluid draining from the ear—

1. Cover the ear lightly with a sterile dressing.

For bleeding around the external ear—

1. Using a dressing, apply pressure to the wound to control bleeding.

For suspected internal ear injury—

1. Seek medical attention.

For a foreign body lodged in the ear—

1. If you can see the object, try to grasp and remove it.
2. Do not try to remove an object with a pin, toothpick or any sharp item.
3. Pull down on the earlobe, tilt the head to the side and shake or gently strike the head on the affected side.
4. If the object does not come out, seek medical assistance.

See also Wounds (p. 179) and Head Neck or Back Injury (p. 135).

► WOUNDS—EMBEDDED OBJECT ◄

An embedded object is any object still in an athlete's wound, whether it is a piece of glass, a knife, or any other object. The object in the wound may be putting pressure on blood vessels that otherwise could cause serious bleeding and therefore should not be removed from the wound. The goals of care are to control bleeding, prevent infection, and minimize shock.

■ WHAT TO DO—

CHECK the scene for safety. **CHECK** the injured athlete, following standard precautions.
CALL 9-1-1 or the local emergency number.
CARE:

1. *Do not* remove the object.
2. Bandage bulky dressings around the object to support the object in place.

3. Bandage the dressing in place.

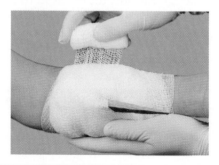

4. Because shock is likely if bleeding is severe, give care to minimize shock (p. 158).

See also Wounds (p. 179).

For an object in the eye, see also Wounds—Eye Injury (see below).

WOUNDS—EYE INJURY

An eye injury may include injury of tissues around the eye, as well as to the eyeball itself. Injuries that penetrate the eyeball are very serious and may cause blindness.

■ WHAT TO LOOK FOR—

- Presence of object or substance in eye
- Pain, burning sensation
- Tears

■ WHAT TO DO—

CHECK the scene for safety. **CHECK** the injured athlete, following standard precautions.

CALL 9-1-1 or the local emergency number if the situation warrants it.

CARE:

For an object embedded in the eye—

1. *Do not* attempt to remove an object embedded in the eye.
2. Place a sterile dressing around the object in the eye; stabilize the object, such as with a *paper* cup, for support.
3. Bandage loosely and *do not* put pressure on the injured eye/eyeball.
4. Seek immediate medical attention.

For small foreign bodies in the eye such as sand or other small debris—

1. Tell the athlete to blink several times to try to remove the object.

2. Gently flush the eye with water.
3. Seek medical attention if the object remains.

For chemical in the eye—

Flush the eye continuously with water for 10 minutes or until EMS personnel arrive. Always flush away from the uninjured eye.

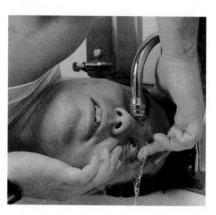

WOUNDS—NOSEBLEED

Nosebleeds are typically caused by a blunt blow to the nose. Bleeding may be heavy at first.

■ WHAT TO DO—

CHECK the scene for safety. **CHECK** the injured athlete, following standard precautions when appropriate.
CALL 9-1-1 or the local emergency number if you suspect a head, neck or back injury or other serious condition.
CARE:
1. Have the athlete sit leaning slightly forward.
2. Pinch the nostrils together for about 10 minutes.
3. Apply an ice pack to the bridge of the nose.

If bleeding does not stop—

4. Apply pressure on the upper lip just beneath the nose.
5. Seek medical attention if the bleeding persists or recurs or if the athlete says it is the result of high blood pressure.
6. Send someone to call EMS personnel if the athlete loses consciousness; position the athlete on the side to allow blood to drain from the nose.

After the bleeding stops—

7. Have the athlete avoid rubbing, blowing, or picking the nose, which could restart the bleeding.
8. Later, with a gloved hand, you may apply petroleum jelly inside the nostril to help keep it moist.

If the injury to the mouth or cheek may be associated with a more serious head, neck or back injury, see Head, Neck or Back Injury (p. 135).

WOUNDS—PUNCTURE

Puncture wounds may be serious because internal tissues may be damaged and because often microorganisms are trapped inside the wound, making infection more likely. Severe bleeding is rare in puncture wounds unless a major blood vessel is injured. The goals of care are to control bleeding and prevent infection.

■ WHAT TO LOOK FOR—

- Red hole in skin
- Redness in area of puncture
- Possible object embedded in wound

■ WHAT TO DO—

CHECK the scene for safety. **CHECK** the injured athlete, following standard precautions.

CALL 9-1-1 or the local emergency number for—

- Bleeding that cannot be stopped.
- Wounds that show muscle or bone, involve joints, gape widely or involve the hands or feet.
- Large or deep wounds.
- Large or deeply embedded objects in the wound. (Do not remove embedded objects.)
- Human or animal bites.
- Any wound that would leave an obvious scar, such as on the face.
- Skin or body parts that have been partially or completely torn away.

CARE:

1. Except for a small object like a splinter, do not remove an embedded object from the wound.
2. Bandage around the object (*see Wounds—Embedded Object, p. 188*).
3. Send someone to call EMS personnel for a serious wound.
4. Cover the wound with a sterile gauze pad and press firmly against the wound. (Use your bare hand to apply pressure only as a last resort.)
5. In cases of serious bleeding, shock is likely; give care to minimize shock (*p. 158*).

If bleeding continues—

6. Use pressure, elevation and bandaging to control the bleeding. Add more dressings as needed. For complete care steps, see *Wounds—Bleeding p. 182*.

If the puncture wound was caused by an object that could carry infection—

Check with a doctor whether a tetanus booster may be needed.

Scalp bleeding may be minor or severe. Although bleeding is usually easily controlled with pressure, be careful in case the skull may be fractured. The goals of care are to recognize a serious injury, get emergency help, and control bleeding.

■ WHAT TO LOOK FOR—

- Bleeding
- Open wound

Signals of skull fracture—

- Depression in the skull
- Spongy feeling of the scalp
- Bone fragments in the wound

■ WHAT TO DO—

CHECK the scene for safety. **CHECK** the injured athlete, following standard precautions when appropriate.
CALL 9-1-1 or the local emergency number if there are signals of a serious condition.
CARE:

1. Apply gentle pressure around the wound over a dressing; feel for the signals of a possible skull fracture.

If there is a risk of a skull fracture—

2. Call 9-1-1 or the local emergency number if you have not already.
3. *Do not* put pressure directly on the wound.
4. Try to control bleeding with pressure on the area around the wound.

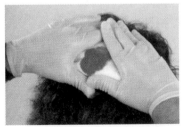

1. Control the bleeding with direct pressure on the dressings.

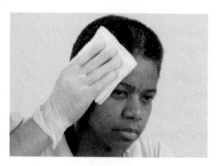

2. Secure dressings in place with a roller bandage.

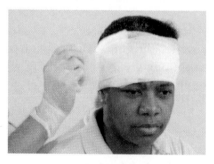

If the scalp injury is associated with a more serious head, neck or back injury, see Head, Neck or Back Injury (*p. 135*).

TOGETHERWE PREPARE

MAKE A PLAN

1. **Talk.** Discover and talk with your family about disasters that can happen where you live. Establish responsibilities for each member of the household and work together as a team. Designate alternates in case someone is absent.

2. **Plan.** Choose two places to meet after a disaster:
   - Right outside your home, in case of a sudden emergency such as a fire.
   - Outside your neighborhood, in case you cannot return home or are asked to evacuate your neighborhood.

3. **Learn.** Each adult in your household should learn how and when to turn off utilities such as electricity, water and gas. Ask someone at the fire department to show you how to use the fire extinguisher you store in your home.

4. **Check supplies.** Review your disaster supplies and replace water and food every six months. (More information on disaster supplies appears in the following section.)

5. **Tell.** Tell everyone in the household where emergency contact information is kept. Make copies for each member to carry with them. Be sure to include an out-of-town contact. It may be easier to call out of the area if local phone lines are overloaded or out of service.

6. **Practice.** Practice evacuating your home twice a year. Drive your planned evacuation route, and plot alternate routes on a map in case main roads are impassible or gridlocked. Practice earthquake, tornado and fire drills at home, school and work. Commit a week-

end every six months to update phone numbers, disaster supplies and review your plan with everyone.

BUILD A KIT

What you have on hand when a disaster happens can make a big difference. Plan on storing enough supplies for everyone in your household for at least three days. Keep these items in an easy to carry container, such as a covered trash container, a large backpack or a duffle bag. Kit basics include:

1. **At least one gallon** of water per person per day.
2. **Non-perishable, high-protein foods**, including energy bars, canned fish and meats, ready-to eat soup, peanut butter, etc. Select foods that require no refrigeration, preparation or cooking and little or no water.
3. **Flashlight with extra batteries.**
4. **Bandages and a first aid kit with a reference guide** such as this *Sport Safety Training Handbook*.
5. **Prescription and non-prescription medications**.
6. **Battery-operated radio with extra batteries.**
7. **Tools:** wrench to turn off gas if necessary (be sure to call your local gas company with any questions regarding your gas service shutoff and appropriate tools), a manual can opener and a screwdriver, hammer, pliers and a knife.
8. **Equipment:** duct tape, plastic sheeting and garbage bags and ties.
9. **Clothing:** a change of clothes for everyone, including sturdy shoes and gloves.
10. **Personal items:** eyeglasses or contact lens and solution; copies of important papers, including identification, insurance policies, birth certificate, passport, etc.; and comfort items such as toys and books.

11. **Sanitary supplies:** toilet paper, towelettes, feminine supplies, personal hygiene items, bleach, etc.
12. **Money:** extra cash and coins (ATMs and credit cards won't work if power is out.).
13. **Contact information:** a current list of family phone numbers and e-mail addresses, including someone out of the area who may be easier to reach if local phone lines are out of service or overloaded.
14. **Pet supplies:** food, water, leash, litter box, tags, any medications and vaccination information.
15. **Map of local area** in case an evacuation is necessary

 GET TRAINED

Properly administered first aid or CPR can help stabilize an injured or ailing person until professional help arrives. Make sure that at least one member of your household is trained in first aid, CPR and how to use an automated external defibrillator (AED), and you'll be able to help anyone, whether in your home, at your job, in your neighborhood or in your community. This quick reference handbook is not a substitute for first aid and CPR/AED training offered by your local Red Cross chapter but provides basic information on the 'get trained' step. To learn more or to contact your local Red Cross chapter, visit the American Red Cross Web site at *www.redcross.org*. Teach children how to dial 9-1-1 in an emergency. Learn the emergency action steps:

- Check the scene and the victim to see if it's safe and assess the cause.
- Call 9-1-1 or your local emergency number and request professional assistance.
- Care for the victim if you can reach the person safely.

Disaster preparedness can provide an additional spectrum of possible responses when emergencies occur. Check with your local American Red Cross chapter for class descriptions, times and costs and information about disaster preparedness presentations.

VOLUNTEER

Every day, the American Red Cross helps people in emergencies . . .whether it's half a million disaster victims or one sick child who needs blood. Our vital work is made possible by people who know how good it can feel to lend a helping hand. Red Cross "everyday heroes" come from all walks of life. Everyone has something special to offer . . . including you.

Last year more than one million Americans helped their communities prevent, prepare for and respond to emergencies as Red Cross volunteers. And the demand for vital American Red Cross services and the committed volunteers to deliver them continues to grow. You can help your community be prepared. To find volunteer opportunities near you, contact your local Red Cross chapter or check out our online database of Red Cross volunteer opportunities with *VolunteerMatch.org*

GIVE BLOOD

America needs a safe and secure blood supply. It is critical to public health. In times of crises, the American Red Cross can quickly ship blood from one area of the country to another—wherever it is needed most. But regular donations of blood are essential to ensure that all needs are met, all of the time. Every two seconds someone in America needs a blood transfusion—cancer patients, accident victims, premature infants, people with chronic diseases. Blood donation means so much to individuals struggling to survive their own personal crisis, and it's something you can do to make a difference.

Giving blood doesn't take much time. Each blood donation has the power to help save as many as three lives. Because whole blood has a shelf life of only 42 days, it is important to be a regular and frequent donor.

Call 1-800-GIVE LIFE (1-800-448-3543) or log on to *www.givelife.org* and make an appointment to donate blood today. Give the Gift of Life: GIVE BLOOD